Santa's Not Going to Clean This!

Quick Pre-Holiday Decluttering for Busy Folks

Table of Contents

CHAPTER 7:   MINIMALIST HOLIDAY DECORATING: HOW TO KEEP YOUR SANITY AND STILL FEEL FESTIVE

CHAPTER 8:   MANAGE TRADITIONAL GIFTS AND GIFT-WRAPPING SUPPLIES

CHAPTER 1:

Decluttering

Let's talk about something that could make your holiday season more joyful and less chaotic than a giant herd of sugar-high reindeer: decluttering.

Picture this: you've just stumbled home after surviving a Black Friday sale, clutching onto your sanity like it's the last discounted TV... only to be greeted by a mountain of wrapping paper, stray socks, and a rogue Christmas wreath that you swore you'd hung up. Instead of a cozy home full of holiday cheer, you wonder if Santa has been secretly dumping his gift rejects there. It's enough to make you cry into your eggnog.

But wait! What if, instead, you walked into a blissfully calm, organized space that practically whispered, "Welcome home, my holiday hero!" Ahhh. Suddenly, the chaos of the world melts away, and you're free to bask in the glow of your clutter-free holiday haven. This, my friend, is why decluttering is your golden ticket to less stress and more festive magic. The holidays are busy enough without your house resembling a reindeer rave at Santa's workshop after. So, let's talk about how to declutter your space—and your mind—so you can focus on the important stuff, like cookies, mostly.

Why Declutter? Because Stress Is About as Festive as Moldy Fruitcake

We've all been there. You're trying to enjoy some holiday cheer, but there's that nagging pile of "stuff" silently judging you from the corner.

You know the one—miscellaneous papers, decorations you *meant* to hang up, and mysterious things you don't even recognize. Clutter doesn't just look bad; it messes with your brain, according to research by Team (2023). It cranks up your stress like a bad holiday tune stuck on repeat.

But here's the secret: you don't have to conquer the whole house at once. Decluttering your entire home in a frenzied cleanup sounds as much fun as organizing your inbox (yep, I went there). So, start small. Think of decluttering like eating a 12-course holiday feast. You wouldn't stuff your face with turkey, mashed potatoes, and pie all at once (unless you're in a competitive eating contest, in which case, good luck). Nope, you take it one delicious bite at a time. Same with decluttering: start small, like one room or drawer. It's less overwhelming; every time you clear a space, it's a tiny victory that feels *so good*. This way, you avoid the dreaded "W*hy did I even start this*?" feeling, and you'll actually see progress. Plus, finding Aunt Edna's missing gift from last year becomes a joyful discovery instead of a hair-pulling scavenger hunt.

The Psychology of Less Clutter: Deck the Halls, Not Your Anxiety Levels

Let's get into the science of why decluttering feels so darn good. First off, a tidy home reduces anxiety. Think of it as turning your living room into a Zen retreat instead of the sad aftermath of a holiday decoration explosion. You'll sleep better, feel better, and hey, you might even have time to finally enjoy some Netflix holiday movies without silently plotting revenge on your Tupperware cabinet. Less mess equals less stress, so you can focus on the important things—like figuring out how to roast that holiday turkey without burning down the kitchen.

Cluttered spaces mess with your focus, making it harder to get anything done—whether it's cooking, decorating, or pretending to be productive at work. The more organized your space, the more you can focus on what actually matters, like perfecting your gingerbread recipe or figuring out where you stashed that ugly Christmas sweater for the next contest.

Productivity? You Bet Your Stockings

When your house is organized, you can find things quickly, saving you precious holiday prep time. No more hunting for the scissors when you're mid-gift-wrap or discovering the turkey baster on Christmas Eve in your partner's toolbox (true story). It's like turning your house into a holiday command center—everything has its place, and you become a gift-wrapping, cookie-baking machine.

Here's a pro tip:

1. Start labeling stuff.

2. Use masking tape, a label maker, or even cheap stick-on labels.

3. Label storage boxes, bins, drawers, and your dog if necessary (kidding, don't do that).

It keeps everything in its proper place and makes you feel like you've unlocked some secret organization superpower. Invest in some simple organizing tools—shelves, drawer dividers, and storage boxes with labels (because hunting for ornaments at the last minute is not the way to enjoy the season). Boom, you've turned your house into a productivity machine and officially won at the holidays.

Decluttering: The Feel-Good Holiday Workout

Decluttering doesn't just make your house look great; it also gives you a weird sense of superhero-level accomplishment. Seriously, there's something magical about clearing out the junk drawer (you know the one) and realizing that you are now *the boss* of your space. It's therapeutic. You might feel an odd but undeniable sense of pride as you toss those old magazines or donate those pleated jeans from the

Dark Ages. Decluttering is basically the adult version of getting a gold star on your holiday to-do list.

It boosts your mood; it does for me. A tidy home is an inviting home. Friends and family can actually enjoy being there, and the whole space will feel more festive without the clutter cramping your holiday vibes. Plus, who doesn't want to host a holiday party in a space that feels *clean and cozy* instead of saying, "Well, I *was* going to clean…"?

How Your Space Messes With Your Mood (And Why Decluttering Fixes It)

The holidays are stressful enough without tripping over random stuff in your hallway and wondering if Santa's elves have been secretly using your dining room for a workshop. You walk into a room, and instead of thinking, "I should really clean that up," you can just chill with a hot cocoa and a cheesy holiday movie. Pure bliss.

Plus, decluttering gives you room for *mindfulness*. You know, those magical moments where you just *exist* without worrying about the 17-plus holiday tasks on your to-do list. You start small—clearing a counter, organizing a shelf, for example—and suddenly, the space (and your brain) feels lighter. It's like you can finally breathe again.

Declutter, Room by Room: The Holiday Edition

Every room in your house deserves some holiday TLC. The bedroom? Make it a clutter-free oasis, and you might actually sleep instead of tossing and turning over holiday stress. The kitchen? Clear the counters, and meal prep will go from "How do I make three side dishes at once?!" to "Look at me; I'm basically a holiday chef now." Each room has its purpose, and decluttering makes them more functional and festive at the same time.

Bonus points for creating zones: Set up a wrapping station, a cozy reading nook, or a hot chocolate bar (you know you want to). These little areas make your home feel extra special for the season, and guests will think you've got it all together.

The Joy of Less: Making Room for Holiday Fun

Decluttering isn't just about getting rid of stuff—it's about making space for what *really* matters. Clear the mess, and suddenly, you've got room to bake cookies with the kids, if you got them, binge-watch holiday movies, or host that Ugly Sweater Party without stress about where people will sit. When your home isn't a cluttered nightmare, you can actually enjoy your favorite holiday traditions without worrying about the mess.

So, this holiday season, do yourself a favor: take a few minutes to declutter and give your home—and your brain—the gift of peace and calm. You'll thank yourself later when you're sipping a hot beverage in a beautifully organized living room instead of frantically searching for lost ornaments. Here's to a less chaotic, more joyful holiday season, one clutter-free space at a time!

For those of you running on coffee and deadlines, there's a simplified, no-nonsense **Chapter Summary for Busy People** after each of the 12 chapters in this book.

Chapter Summary for Busy People

- **Decluttering reduces holiday stress**
  - A clutter-free home creates a serene, relaxing environment, reducing sensory overload and stress.
  - Coming home to an organized space makes it easier to unwind after holiday errands or work.
- **Psychological benefits**

-       ○ Decluttering clears mental clutter, reduces anxiety, and enhances focus.

  ○ A clean home promotes productivity, making holiday preparations smoother.

- **Start small and build progress**

  ○ Tackle clutter one room, corner, or drawer at a time to avoid feeling overwhelmed.

  ○ Celebrate small victories as you declutter each space.

- **Productivity boost**

  ○ An organized home saves time and energy by making it easier to find holiday items like decorations and kitchen tools.

  ○ Use organizational tools like shelves, drawer dividers, and labeled storage to keep things tidy.

- **Sense of accomplishment**

  ○ Decluttering fosters a feeling of control and achievement.

  ○ It can be therapeutic, transforming your space into a place of pride.

- **Impact on well-being**

  ○ A decluttered home improves mood, sleep, and emotional stability.

  ○ Organized spaces like kitchens or bedrooms enhance creativity and relaxation.

- **Creating functional zones**

  ○ Establish zones for specific activities, such as gift wrapping or cozy reading nooks.

- o Define areas for family gatherings to encourage meaningful interactions.

- **Boosting holiday enjoyment**
  - o A clutter-free environment creates space for holiday decorations and activities without feeling cramped.
  - o A clean home becomes a welcoming space for friends and family gatherings.

- **Mindfulness and connection**
  - o Decluttering shifts your focus from material things to meaningful experiences.
  - o Spend less time cleaning and more time connecting with loved ones.

- **Creating room for festive activities**
  - o Decluttering facilitates gatherings, maximizes space for holiday activities, and fosters creativity.
  - o It encourages connection, reduces stress, and allows more quality time with family and friends.

CHAPTER 2:

Declutter for the Holidays— The Battle for Sanity

Welcome to the holidays, my brave warrior! This book is specifically for decluttering before and after the holidays. Many of the ideas in the following chapters can and should be used year-round. Let's get to it.

The season of joy, *togethermess*, (sorry, togetherness), and—oh yes—clutter that multiplies faster than fruitcakes no one asked for. You've got family coming, presents to wrap, and kids bouncing off the walls and sticking to the wooden floors from a caramel apple high. Your house? It looks like your Christmas tree had a serious case of the flu and regurgitated everything Christmas. But fear not, fellow festive friend! With this foolproof declutter plan, you'll transform your home from "yikes" to "Pinterest-perfect" faster than you can say, "Where the heck is the tape?!"

In this chapter, we will give you a brief idea or summary of how to turn your clutter into organized bliss. Think of it as turning your house from "How did we lose a whole couch under this stuff?" to "Wow, is this a photo shoot for *Better Living Through Decluttering?*" If you are anxious to begin, the following chapters provide more detailed ideas for decluttering rooms, closets, cabinets, and drawers and the practical tools to accomplish your goals.

Grab your cocoa—or if the kids are extra hyper, maybe something stronger—and let's dive in. We've got goals to set, clutter hotspots to tackle, and a battle plan to form. But don't worry, this isn't boot camp. It's more like an adventure through your home, with a lot less crying, hopefully.

Setting Realistic Goals and Timelines

Okay, so let's start with a truth bomb: setting goals during the holidays is like herding cats while trying to wrap gifts with one hand. It's a lot of chaos, a lot of noise, and maybe some tears. But fear not! With the right plan, you can declutter your home faster than you can say, "Did our Christmas tree catch the flu again?"

The first step in this decluttering adventure is setting realistic goals. And by realistic, I don't mean "clean the entire house in one afternoon." No, we're talking about breaking this task into small, manageable bites, like nibbling on a gingerbread cookie instead of shoving the whole thing in your mouth and regretting it later. You're not a wizard, Declutter Daphne, and there's no wand that'll make the clutter disappear, though if someone invents one, please send it my way.

Establish Specific Goals: "Santa's Workshop or Tornado Aftermath?"

Specific goals are your new best friend. Let's be honest: if your decluttering goal is vague, like cleaning the house, you are doomed from the start. It's like saying you're going to run a marathon but then realizing you haven't even put on shoes yet.

Let's get specific. Pick an area, any area, and start there. For example, you could tackle the entryway. This high-traffic zone is probably where sad shoes, coats, backpacks, and random Amazon packages gather to form a small mountain. You know the one I'm talking about—the mini-Everest of a mess that greets you whenever you walk through the door.

Now, instead of something vague like "clean the entryway," try decluttering the shoe pile and organizing the coat rack. Boom! It's specific, achievable, and not overwhelming. You'll be channeling your inner mess mercenary in no time.

Remember, these specific goals are like kids who know they have to raise their grades to avoid "the talk" with their parents. It's all about focus, determination, and a little fear (Engebretson, 2024).

Create a Timeline: "The Holiday Cheat Sheet You Never Knew You Needed"

Timelines are like magic—except, you know, real. Setting a timeline for your decluttering tasks is your secret weapon for avoiding procrastination. You'll hustle like never before when you know you've got only 30 minutes to clean up the kitchen before you collapse on the couch to watch another cheesy movie.

Think of your timeline as a holiday cheat sheet, laying out when each cleanup session happens. I'm not saying you need to schedule every minute of your life (leave room for music breaks), but penciling in some decluttering sessions between Thanksgiving feasts and post-present naps will keep you from drowning in last-minute chaos (Kmattison, 2023).

Start by scheduling a decluttering blitz for each room of the house. Maybe Monkey Bread Monday is for the kitchen because who doesn't want to clean up spilled flour everywhere and dry bread batter on the counters? Tuesday is for the living room. RIP to that bowl of popcorn from 2 days ago. Wednesday is for the guest room, so Aunt Mildred has a place to sleep that doesn't involve an inflatable mattress.

Set Daily or Weekly Tasks

We all love the idea of getting everything done in one fell swoop, but here's a little reality check: you're not a superhero (though you do look great in that apron). Decluttering your home takes time. But that's okay! Rome wasn't built in a day, and neither is your clutter-free kingdom.

Pro tip: Reward yourself for these small victories. Decluttering the living room? Have a cookie. Clearing off the kitchen counter? Another cookie. It's a scientifically proven fact—okay, maybe not scientific, but go with me here—that cookies make everything better (Loves, 2019).

Acknowledge Progress: "The Holiday Decluttering Victory Lap"

I get it—decluttering isn't exactly a glamorous activity, but when you start to make progress, you'll feel like a million bucks. Seriously, there's something incredibly satisfying about checking things off a list, especially when that list started as a mountain of "to-dos."

Keep a visible checklist somewhere you can see it, like on the fridge or taped to your forehead (just kidding, kind of). As you complete each task, mark it off. Each time you cross something out, it'll feel like scoring a touchdown in the Super Bowl.

Celebrating small wins along the way can turn a daunting decluttering marathon into a fun, rewarding challenge. You could even rope in your friends or family for some good-natured competition. Who can declutter their room the fastest? Who can find the most random item buried under the clutter? (Winner gets extra dessert, obviously.) Just like that, you've turned decluttering from a chore into a full-blown holiday competition (Manneh, 2019).

Identify High-Clutter Zones in Your Home

Now that we've tackled goal setting, it's time to take a good, hard look at your home. No judgment here—we all have those clutter zones that are more "accumulation station" than "First Lady-approved." But to win this battle, you need to know your enemy. And in this case, your enemy is the clutter lurking in every nook and cranny.

Assess Common Clutter Areas: "The Usual Suspects"

When you're looking for clutter, start with the usual suspects. You know the ones: the entryway that looks like a shoe explosion, the kitchen counter covered in everything but food, and the coffee table that's less of a "table" and more of a "storage unit for remote controls, magazines, six different mugs, and—wait, is that a caramel apple core?!"

Think about it. Clutter breeds in the places you spend the most time. It's like dust bunnies—they always show up where you least expect them and multiply overnight. The entryway, the living room, and the kitchen are classic clutter hotspots because that's where the action happens. If you tackle these high-traffic areas, you'll make a serious dent in the mess (Holistic Decluttering Methods, 2023).

Conduct a Room-By-Room Evaluation: "Channel Your Inner Detective"

It's time to go full Sherlock Holmes. Grab a magnifying glass—or just your regular glasses—and do a room-by-room walkthrough of your home. As you inspect each space, ask yourself: "What's the clutter culprit in here?" Is it the pile of clothes that never made it to the laundry? Are the books stacked high enough to double as a Jenga tower? Or is it just a general sense that your belongings have slowly taken over your life?

Make notes as you go—mental or physical, depending on how ambitious you're feeling—and prioritize the rooms that need the most attention. And if you feel like you're auditioning for a home makeover show, don't worry. You're just a step away from your big decluttering breakthrough.

The Four-Box Method: "Sorting Like a Holiday Pro"

Now comes the fun part: decluttering! And by fun, I mean, "Oh wow, I forgot I owned this," which is surprisingly satisfying. Enter the Four-Box Method—your new best friend and a friend referred to often in this book.

Here's the deal: grab four boxes or bags and label them "Keep," "Donate," "Discard," and "Relocate." It's like throwing a holiday party for your clutter, but only the cool stuff gets to stay.

Keep: These are the items that you actually use and love, and no, that doesn't include the sweater your great-aunt knitted for you in 1997 that moths used as a snack in 2002. The "keep" box should be your smallest box because the goal here is not to keep everything— it's to only keep the good stuff. Think of this box as a VIP lounge for your favorite belongings. The rest? Not so lucky.

Donate: This is where all those clothes, toys, and random kitchen gadgets you don't need anymore go to find a new home. You're not throwing them out—you're giving them a second chance at life, probably in someone else's cluttered home. Just kidding! But seriously, it's the season of giving, so why not clear your clutter while helping someone else?

Discard: You know that drawer of random cords that don't fit any devices you own? Yeah, those go in the discard box. The same goes for anything broken, torn, or otherwise unsalvageable. This is where the true holiday magic happens—by tossing the junk, you're making space for all the things that actually matter (or for new holiday gifts that will inevitably arrive).

Relocate: Ah, the "I don't belong here" box. This box is for items that have somehow wandered into the wrong room, like the laundry basket hanging out in the living room or the pile of mail taking up space on your kitchen counter. Relocating is like putting things back where they belong—because your house apparently didn't have a self-organizing feature.

Once you've filled your boxes, get moving. Drop off the donations, throw out the discards, and put away those wandering items before they reproduce.

Recognize the Underlying Causes of Clutter: " Why Do We Do This to Ourselves?"

Now that you've made a serious dent in the clutter, let's talk about the why. Why do we always end up with so much stuff? Why does every holiday season bring a fresh wave of junk into our homes like a festive tsunami?

In my case, there are a few reasons, but the big ones are impulse shopping and a general lack of organization. The holidays are prime time for both. It's easy to get swept up in the spirit of the season and suddenly find yourself surrounded by bags of stuff you didn't know you needed but couldn't resist. And once that stuff arrives in your home, it quickly finds its way into piles, closets, and corners, where it breeds more clutter like rabbits at a family reunion.

The key to avoiding future clutter and mess is understanding these triggers and putting systems in place to stop them in their tracks. This could mean setting a shopping limit, adopting a "one in, one out" rule (where for every new item you bring home, something old must go), or simply resisting the urge to buy a life-sized ceramic penguin just because it's 40% off. You know the penguin I'm talking about. We've all been there.

Evaluate Items by Frequency of Use: "When Was the Last Time I Actually Used This?"

Maybe some of the stuff cluttering your house hasn't seen the light of day since the Clinton administration. It's time to get ruthless and evaluate items based on how often you use them. If it hasn't been touched in over a year (and it's not something seasonal like holiday decorations), it's probably safe to say you can live without it.

Take that exercise bike in the corner, for example. If the last time somebody used it was when you swore to start a New Year's resolution in 2016, it's probably time to say goodbye. I'm sure it'll make a lovely coat rack for someone else.

Decluttering high-traffic areas first—like your kitchen, living room, and bedroom—will give you the biggest payoff. Not only will it feel amazing to clear those spaces, but it'll also make you feel like you're gaining momentum. Like shedding those five extra holiday pounds you somehow gained before even eating Thanksgiving dinner, decluttering these areas gives you immediate relief (Manneh, 2019).

Assess the Emotional Impact of Items: "Does This Spark Joy—or Just a Mild Headache?"

Let's take a moment to talk about feelings—specifically, your feelings toward your clutter. Some of the stuff in your house might not be useful, but it holds sentimental value. That's fine until it's not. At some point, you have to decide whether these emotional attachments are worth the space they're taking up.

For example, are you holding onto that box of old love letters from high school because they remind you of a simpler time, or are they just keeping you stuck in the past? No judgment if you're still waiting for that guy who sat behind you in chemistry to call. We've all been there.

The idea is to recognize what emotionally heavy items are doing to your space and your mindset. It might be time to part ways if they're causing more stress than joy. A good rule of thumb is the Marie Kondo method: if it doesn't spark joy, it's got to go. And let's be real: if it sparks anxiety, it's definitely out the door.

Implement the 20/20 Rule: "Letting Go With Confidence"

Here's a great little rule for helping you let go of clutter without having a full-blown existential crisis: the 20/20 rule. If an item costs less than $20 and takes less than 20 minutes to replace, get rid of it. This rule is like the clutter-buster version of "just say no." It's liberating!

Think of it this way: how many times have you held onto something "just in case" you might need it in the future? Chances are, you don't need 27 empty yogurt containers, and you definitely don't need that dusty set of VHS tapes from your childhood (unless you have a functioning VCR, in which case, congratulations on your time travel device).

The 20/20 rule helps you ditch the clutter guilt-free. If it's cheap and easy to replace, you won't even miss it (Kmattison, 2023).

Focus on Entryways and Common Areas First: "The Holiday Clutter Frontline"

When it comes to decluttering, first impressions matter. Your entryway is the first thing guests see when they walk in (and the first thing you trip over when you come home), so it's a great place to start.

You'll create an immediate impact by tackling the entryway and other common areas like the living room. Plus, you'll be less likely to fall victim to random piles of shoes, umbrellas, and mysteriously abandoned mail. Bonus points if you finally find your keys buried under that pile of scarves.

And hey, once the entryway is cleared, you'll feel motivated to keep going. It's like winning the first round of a video game—now you're ready to face the next level of clutter. Just remember, every step you take in decluttering is a step closer to holiday bliss.

Communicate the Importance of Decluttering: "It's Not Just for Your Sanity—It's for Everyone's Sanity"

Let's face it: getting your family involved in decluttering is like getting everyone to agree on a flick for family movie night. Someone's going to resist, someone's going to complain, and someone's probably going to hide in their room until it's over. But involving the whole family is vital to lightening your load and making the process faster—and, dare I say, fun?

Start by explaining the importance of decluttering to your family. Make it clear that a tidy home means less stress for everyone, more space for holiday decorations, and—most importantly—a better place to hide gifts from nosy kids. Plus, you can always offer rewards for cooperation, like pizza for dinner or movie night after the decluttering session.

Once everyone's on board—or at least pretending to be—you'll be ready to tackle the holiday clutter together.

Set Clear Roles and Responsibilities: "Divide and Conquer the Clutter Beast"

Decluttering is much easier when everyone has a role to play. Trying to do it all yourself is a surefire way to end up in a pile of ribbon roles and broken ornaments, softly weeping as tears flow into your "hard" eggnog.

Instead, assign tasks based on everyone's strengths. Kids can handle sorting through toys and books, while your partner can take on the garage or basement (because no one should have to go down there alone). The key is to set clear responsibilities so everyone feels they're contributing to the decluttering mission.

Incorporate Fun Activities or Rewards: "Turn Decluttering Into a Game"

Decluttering doesn't have to feel like a chore, especially during the holidays when everyone's already in the mood for fun and games. Why not turn the decluttering process into an activity the whole family enjoys? Here are a few ideas to get everyone excited about pitching in:

Make it a competition: Who can declutter their space the fastest? Set a timer, and let each family member tackle a different area. The winner gets a holiday treat or first dibs on watching the next family holiday movie.

Create a scavenger hunt: List items that need to be found and sorted (like holiday decorations, missing socks, or mysterious keys). Whoever finds and organizes the most wins.

Reward with treats or breaks: Declutter one room? Time for a kiss and a hug. Finished the whole house? Celebrate with a hot cocoa party or a holiday movie marathon, and the winner gets to wear the tinsel garland crown. Rewards give everyone a little extra motivation.

By making the process fun and adding rewards, your family will be more willing to pitch in. Plus, it can turn what might feel like a tedious task into a holiday memory of working together.

Maintain a Decluttered Home: "The Final Frontier"

Now that you've battled the clutter and won, the challenge is keeping it that way. With the holidays in full swing, new gifts, decorations, and holiday cards are bound to arrive and stir up the clutter again. But don't worry—there are strategies to help you maintain the peace you've worked so hard to create.

Implement Daily Habits: "Tidy in 10"

If you're not careful, clutter will sneak back in faster than your cat can knock over the Christmas poinsettia. But by setting aside just 10 minutes daily to tidy up, you can keep things from getting out of control.

Pick a time—morning, before bed, or after dinner—and use those 10 minutes to clear high-clutter zones like the entryway, kitchen counters, or living room. Daily cleaning of these spaces will prevent them from turning into disaster zones.

Seasonal Maintenance: "Out With the Old, In With the New"

After the holidays, take time to evaluate your holiday items before packing them away. Did you use all those ornaments this year? Are you hanging onto decorations that no longer fit your style? If something didn't make the cut this season, consider donating it instead of putting it back into storage.

Likewise, when the gift-giving bonanza is over, take stock of what you've received. If there are things you won't use or don't need, there's no harm in exchanging or donating them. Remember, one person's "meh" gift could be someone else's perfect find.

Decluttering Mindset: "A Lifestyle, Not a Seasonal Fix"

Decluttering isn't just a one-time event, especially around the holidays when havoc tends to creep back in every year. The goal is to adopt a decluttering mindset—a lifestyle of keeping things organized, simplified, and under control.

Understand the Emotional Benefits of Decluttering: "Joy Isn't Just in the Stuff"

Once you've cleared the clutter, you'll likely find that your stress levels drop, your home feels more inviting, and you have more time to relax and enjoy the holidays. Decluttering brings emotional freedom, giving you more headspace and less anxiety about the piles of stuff.

When your surroundings are clear and calm, you set the tone for the rest of your life. The holidays can be stressful enough, but with a decluttered home, you can truly focus on what matters—time with loved ones, meaningful traditions, and enjoying the season.

Establish Boundaries With New Items: "Don't Let the Stuff Win"

The holidays often bring a flood of new items, from gifts to decorations. To prevent the clutter from coming back, set boundaries for what enters your home. For every new gift or decoration, consider removing something old. As mentioned before, this "one in, one out" rule is a powerful way to keep things from getting overwhelming again.

And don't be afraid to say "no" to items that don't serve a purpose or bring joy. Just because it's a gift doesn't mean it needs to take up permanent residence in your home (sorry, light-up reindeer sweater).

Conclusion: Declutter Your Way to a Joyful, Calm Holiday Season

Congratulations—you've survived the great holiday decluttering extravaganza and set yourself up for a more peaceful, joyful season. There will be no more last-minute panic about where to put guests or digging through piles of wrapping paper for that one missing gift.

You've reclaimed your home from the chaos by setting realistic goals, identifying clutter hotspots, involving your family, and maintaining daily habits. And while the holidays may bring in more stuff, you now have the tools to keep things under control.

The best part? You can truly enjoy your home again without feeling drowning in a sea of seasonal knick-knacks. So grab that eggnog, sit back, and marvel at the beautifully decluttered space you'll create. Here's to a calm, joyful, and clutter-free holiday season!

Chapter Summary for Busy People

- Holiday chaos: The holidays bring joy, togetherness, and clutter that grows out of control—family, gifts, and sticky floors are just the beginning.

- Decluttering strategy: Follow a simple decluttering plan to transform your home from messiness to organized bliss. Tackle key areas step by step.

- Setting realistic goals: Break tasks into smaller, manageable steps. No magic wands here—start with specific, bite-sized goals, like "organize the coat rack."

- Time management: Use timelines to avoid procrastination. Set decluttering "appointments" for each room—kitchen on Monday, living room on Tuesday, etc.

- Daily or weekly tasks: Focus on small wins each day. Even 10 minutes of decluttering adds up and keeps things manageable.

- Identify high-clutter zones: Start with common areas that accumulate clutter, like the entryway, kitchen, and living room. Prioritize based on where the mess builds up fastest. The Four-Box Method: Sort items into four boxes: Keep, Donate, Discard, and Relocate. Make decisions quickly and act on them immediately.

- Assess the emotional impact: If it doesn't spark joy or cause stress, let it go. Don't keep things "just in case."

- Involve family: Get everyone in on the decluttering game. Assign tasks, make it fun, and offer rewards for participation.

- Maintain decluttered spaces: Commit to daily 10-minute tidying sessions to keep clutter at bay, especially in high-traffic areas.

- Set boundaries with new items: For every new gift or holiday item, consider donating or discarding something old to keep clutter under control.

Enjoy the Benefits: A decluttered home means less stress, more peace, and the freedom to enjoy the holidays with loved ones.

CHAPTER 3

Declutter the Living Room: The Heart of Holiday Gatherings

Ah, the living room—the stage for all your festive gatherings and cozy holiday memories. It's where we drink eggnog, exchange awkward presents, and dodge political conversations. But before you deck the halls and perfect your holiday playlist, you've got to tackle the mess that has taken over your living room. Because let's face it: while it's the heart of holiday cheer, it's also the battlefield of everyday life, where clutter reigns supreme. Piles of magazines, socks, that bag you swore you'd take to the gym, and random cat, dog, or kids' toys underfoot— it's like your personal Bermuda Triangle of everything misplaced (Poplin, 2019).

Fear not, intrepid holiday host! I'm here to guide you on a step-by-step adventure to declutter your living room, transforming it from a frenzied mess into a holiday haven. Think of it as less of a chore and more of a home makeover show—except you're the star, and the prize is sanity. So, grab your coffee (or mulled wine, no judgment), and let's get to work.

The War on Clutter: Surface Attacks

Picture this: your in-laws are due to arrive in an hour. You've got cookies in the oven, a sparkling tree, and—what's that? Your coffee table is drowning in yesterday's junk mail and three mugs of cold coffee—cue panic. Cluttered surfaces are like magnets for mess that multiply faster than feral cats on the prowl. You had such visions of cozy, festive family gatherings, yet here you are, one junk pile away from being an episode on *Hoards, In-Law Edition*. Fear not, my budding Jedi. We are about to embark on a journey to transfer your living room from a battlefield of clutter into a warm, inviting space of holiday magic (Poplin, 2019).

Step One: Clear the Coffee Table

First, let's tackle the coffee table—a notorious clutter zone. It's where half-read magazines go to die, remote controls have meetings, and coffee mugs have a secret convention. First, grab a basket (or a small box if you're fancy) and sweep every item into it. Yes, everything. Your coffee table should look like the minimalist dream you once pinned on Pinterest (Better Homes & Gardens, n.d.). You'll rediscover its smooth surface and maybe even feel a sense of inner peace. Or at least enough calm to make it through dinner.

Once you've gathered all the items, you can categorize trash, things to keep, and things that belong elsewhere. And here's the kicker—only keep things that either add to your holiday aesthetic or serve a practical purpose. That stack of catalogs? Recycle. The five remotes? Two-word solution: universal remote. And if you can't bear to part with your holiday-scented candles, at least limit it to one or two (I'm looking at you, "Cinnamon Spice" and "Winter Wonderland").

Once the coffee table is clear, give it a good wipe-down. There's something magical about seeing your coffee table again, gleaming like it just got a makeover on one of those home renovation shows (Kerr, 2022). Anything that stays should serve a purpose or add to your holiday aesthetic. If it doesn't, it's time to temporarily send it packing.

> **Pro tip:** Designate a permanent home for your remotes and other frequently used items—a stylish basket for remote controls, a small decorative coaster tray, or a cute jar for stray coins (Better Homes & Gardens, n.d.). These small touches add intentionality and style, all while preventing clutter that often seems like it's offering free snacks to lure random objects. You can reclaim your coffee table from the mess and give it the dignity it deserves.

Underfoot Hazards: Avoiding the Shoe-Toy Trap

Now, let's talk about your floor. Living rooms can be a landmine of shoes, various animal or human toys, and, of course, that stray sock you're starting to believe belongs to the universe now. There's nothing like tripping over a Lego while delivering a plate of Christmas cookies to your in-laws to really kill the festive vibe (and your foot) (Poplin, 2019). Avoid holiday bloopers by tackling these underfoot hazards with some creative solutions.

Step Two: Corral the Chaos

First, let's address the footwear situation. Shoes have a way of multiplying when you're not looking. That pair of boots by the door? It invited sneakers, slippers, and flip-flops to the party. Use a shoe rack or basket near the entryway to create a designated shoe zone. This gives everyone a place to drop their shoes that isn't in the middle of the room—plus, you won't have to play detective to find your missing boot (Martha Stewart, n.d.).

As for toys, those need a containment plan. Use storage bins or decorative baskets to corral kids' toys in a way that's easy to clean up and looks intentional. Bonus points if the baskets match your holiday decor (imagine a chic wicker basket hiding a mountain of action figures—so festive). And if you can convince the kids to make a game out of cleaning up, even better. Just don't trip over the toy bins because irony hurts.

> **Pro tip:** Stash toys that aren't holiday-themed in a closet or spare room until after the festivities—out of sight, out of mind—and out of your way.

Personal Items: Save the Knickknacks for Later

We all have them: those quirky little knickknacks that make our homes feel like "us." But when holiday decor takes center stage, your random owl figurine or that framed photo of you awkwardly hugging a llama might not exactly scream "festive" (Poplin, 2019). This is where decluttering gets a bit personal—literally.

Step Three: Dial Back the Everyday Decor

Holiday decor should be the star of the show, so it's time to put some of your regular Knickknacks on hiatus. Start by selecting a few key personal items to keep on display—your favorite family photo or that quirky heirloom from Grandma. The rest? Give them a vacation (Better Homes & Gardens, n.d.).

For example, if your mantel is currently a shrine to miscellaneous family mementos, pare it down. Leave one- or two-family photos, and let your garland or stockings take center stage (Kerr, 2022). Paring down creates balance and allows the holiday magic to shine.

> **Pro tip:** When it comes to holiday decor, less is often more. Don't feel you need to display every ornament you've ever owned. Choose a holiday theme and color palette and stick to it—you'll have a more cohesive (and less cluttered) holiday look (Kerr, 2022).

Entertainment Systems: From Chaos to Control

The entertainment center is another hot spot for clutter. Between cords, remote controls, game consoles, and DVDs (yes, some of us still have those), it's easy for things to get out of hand. Before you know it, your entertainment system looks more like a tech graveyard than a place to binge-watch your favorite holiday movies (Martha Stewart, n.d.).

Step Four: Tame the Technology

First things first—let's wrangle the cords. Cords are the bane of a clutter-free living room, so take the time to untangle and organize them. Use cord clips or cable management boxes to keep them neat and out of sight. Label all cords to avoid confusion later on when you're trying to figure out which one belongs to the TV and which one charges your ancient gaming console (https://www.facebook.com/realsimple, 2021).

Next, consolidate your remotes—yes, all of them. Invest in a universal remote if you're still juggling four or five. It'll make your life easier and your coffee table less cluttered. Store all game controllers, DVDs, and other accessories in decorative baskets or bins. These containers keep everything within reach but out of sight, adding a layer of organization that still looks stylish (Better Homes & Gardens, n.d.).

> **Pro tip:** If you're up for it, consider mounting your TV on the wall. It will free up space on your entertainment console and add a sleek, modern look to the room. Just hide the cords for a seamless finish (Martha Stewart, n.d.).

Seasonal Decor: Less Is More

It's easy to go overboard when it comes to holiday decorating—especially if you have a collection of sentimental ornaments, stockings, and festive trinkets. But here's the truth: less is more. A living room drowning in garlands, figurines, and twinkling lights can feel overwhelming rather than cozy (Kerr, 2022).

Step Five: Edit Your Holiday Decor

The key to tasteful holiday decorating is balance. Let's begin by selecting a color palette or theme for your decor. Whether it's a classic red and green motif, a winter wonderland in whites and silvers, or a cozy rustic vibe, sticking to a theme helps create a cohesive look that feels intentional (Better Homes & Gardens, n.d.).

As you decorate, think about layers—starting with the bigger items like your tree, stockings, and garlands, then adding smaller accent pieces. Avoid overcrowding surfaces like your mantel, coffee table, or bookshelves. These should be decorated with intention, not cluttered with every holiday knickknack you own (Kerr, 2022).

> **Pro tip:** Pack away non-holiday decor to make room for your seasonal items. For example, swap out your everyday throw pillows for festive ones and put away any artwork or photos that don't match your holiday theme (Poplin, 2019).

Storage Solutions: Pack It Away

You're left with one final task when the holidays are over: packing it all away. How you store your holiday decorations can make or break your decluttering success for future seasons (https://www.facebook.com/realsimple, 2021).

Step Six: Organize Your Storage

The key to efficient holiday storage is to be strategic. Use clear, labeled bins for easy identification next year, and store items like ornaments, garlands, and lights in designated containers to prevent tangling or damage (Better Homes & Gardens, n.d.). Make sure to store your bins in a place that's easy to access so you're not dreading next year's decorating duties. Consider using vacuum-sealed bags for bulky items like stockings, tree skirts, or holiday linens. These can be compressed for easy storage and take up far less space in your attic or closet (Martha Stewart, n.d.).

> **Pro tip:** Keep an inventory, using a journal or festive notebook, of your holiday decorations and what box they're in. Using a journal or festive notebook may sound like overkill, but next year, when you're

hunting for that one specific ornament or strand of lights, you'll be so happy you did!

From Clutter to Comfort

Decluttering your living room doesn't just make space for your holiday decorations—it makes space for joy, relaxation, and all the memories you'll create during the season. Following these steps, you can transform your living room from chaotic to cozy, ensuring it's a welcoming environment for guests and a sanctuary for yourself.

With the mess cleared and the decorations up, you're now ready to kick back, relax, and actually—just the holidays. No more tripping over shoes or searching for remotes. Just you, your family, and a cozy, clutter-free space filled with warmth and cheer.

So, put on your favorite holiday movie, pour yourself a cup of cocoa, and bask in the satisfaction of a job well done.

Chapter Summary for Busy People

- **Declutter the surfaces**
    - Start with the obvious—clear off surfaces like coffee tables, bookshelves, and mantels.
    - Use trays, baskets, or decorative bowls to contain small items (Martha Stewart, n.d.).
- **Create storage for everyday items**
    - Add stylish storage solutions like baskets, bins, or ottomans with hidden storage.
    - Designate a place for blankets, magazines, and remote controls (Better Homes & Gardens, n.d.).
- **Tame the technology**

   ○ Organize and label cords; hide them with cable management boxes or clips.

   ○ Consolidate remotes with a universal remote, and store controllers and DVDs in decorative bins (https://www.facebook.com/realsimple, 2021).

- **Less is more with holiday decor**

   ○ Pick a holiday theme or color palette and stick to it for a cohesive look.

   ○ Avoid overcrowding—swap out non-holiday items for seasonal decor to keep things balanced (Kerr, 2022).

- **Pack away holiday items efficiently**

   ○ Use clear, labeled bins for holiday decor and vacuum-sealed bags for bulky items.

   ○ Keep an inventory of your decorations for easier setup next year (Poplin, 2019).

CHAPTER 4:

Streamline the Kitchen: Preparing for Festive Feasts (Without Losing Your Mind)

Ah, the kitchen. It's the heart of the home, the command center, the battlefield where snacks are inhaled, and questionable leftovers go to… well, nobody really knows. As the holidays approach, this space can be your greatest ally or worst enemy. Right now, it probably feels like the latter, with countertops that look like they've seen more action than a reality show reunion. But fear not! We're about to turn this area into a smooth, efficient, festive culinary wonderland (CoCo, 2023).

First things first, let's talk pantry and fridge—aka, the enablers of expired food. These two spots are basically where grocery items go to disappear, never to be seen again until they've reached a level of fermentation that even science can't explain. Have you ever found a jar of salsa in the back of the fridge with its own ecosystem? Yeah, we're going to fix that (Cook, 2023).

Step one: Take a deep breath and open your pantry. Now, try not to faint. If you're like most people, it's probably filled with 37 half-empty bags of chips, 12 kinds of flour (why do you have so much flour?), and canned goods from the era when dinosaurs roamed the earth. Brace yourself. We're going in.

Time for an Inventory Sweep

This is where you ruthlessly ditch anything expired or that "sounded like a good idea at the time" but hasn't seen the light of day since. Quinoa pasta? It's time for a heart-to-heart about why you thought that would change your life. All you are doing is pitching expired products at this point—baby steps (Mindful Decluttering & Organizing, 2019).

Fridge? Same Deal

Start by pulling out everything that has expired while confronting your life choices. Why do you have three bottles of ketchup? Where did that random jar of expired artichoke hearts come from? And does that greenish yogurt have *feelings* now? Do an inventory of what's fresh and what's auditioning for the next season of "Stranger Things," and toss anything questionable (or anything that gives you side-eye). After cleaning the countertops, we will pull everything out of the refrigerator and pantry in the next step.

Next Up, Countertops

Right now, your countertops probably resemble an archaeological dig—layers of stuff piled high with no clear purpose. But imagine this: countertops that are both functional and festive. It's possible, I promise. First, clear the decks. Remove all the random gadgets you thought you'd use (I'm looking at you, avocado slicer), the bowls of fruit that turned into bowls of mush, and the mail you've meant to sort for months. Only keep out what you'll actually need for cooking or holiday cheer (CoCo, 2023).

Once you've cleared the clutter, bring in some festive flair. A holiday-themed dishtowel here, a pine-scented candle there—voilà, you've got yourself a holiday kitchen that would make even Santa nod in approval. Just don't go overboard and start hanging tinsel on your spice rack.

We're going for "festive," not "tons of tinsel exploded in an atomic mushroom cloud." (Cook, 2023).

Let's Talk Storage

This is where you and bins, baskets, and containers become BFFs. Picture this: instead of every drawer being a mish-mash land of misfit gadgets, everything has a designated place. Your spatulas aren't fighting for space with your measuring cups. Your spices are in neat little jars, not scattered across three different cabinets (Stamp, 2020). Sounds dreamy, right? That's because it is. Get yourself some stackable containers and labels for dry goods. When we get to organizing, we will be labeling them so you actually know what's in them. Trust me, in the future, you will be very grateful when you're not playing "Guess what this unlabeled powder is" while baking cookies.

Bonus Points for Using Festive Containers

Think red and green bins for organizing pantry items or holiday-themed baskets for storing snacks. It's both practical and cute, and suddenly, you're living in a world where holiday magic meets organizational bliss. Not only does this help keep things tidy, but it also means you won't accidentally end up with four bags of powdered sugar because you keep forgetting you already bought some—been there! (Prochefkitchentools.com, n.d.).

By the end of this decluttering and organizing extravaganza, you'll be able to walk into your kitchen, take a deep breath, and actually enjoy the space without feeling like it's judging you. Plus, with everything in order, you'll have more room to focus on what really matters: preparing those epic holiday feasts, jamming to your favorite tunes, and maybe even sneaking a glass of wine (or two) while the turkey roasts (Vertical Spice, 2024).

So, grab that apron, blast some holiday tunes, and let's turn this kitchen from a cluttered catastrophe to an organized, festive heaven. And who knows? You might even *enjoy* cooking this year by the time we're done. (Okay, let's not get crazy.)

Organizing Pantry and Fridge to Reduce Food Waste

We've tossed the expired food products in our pantry and fridge, and our countertops are clutter-free! We are well on our way to being almost superhuman! Time now for the next baby step: organizing. This section will guide you in efficiently organizing your kitchen storage areas, aiming to minimize food waste and create a functional cooking space that even grandmother would approve of (Mindful Decluttering & Organizing, 2019).

Before you channel your inner chef extraordinaire, take stock of what you already have in your pantry and fridge. It's time to find out what's lurking in the depths of your pantry and fridge. Think of it as a treasure hunt—except instead of gold; you're searching for that ancient can of beans you were *sure* you bought three years ago. It's a surprise party, but the guests are long-forgotten food items—dusty bags of flour, half-empty sauce jars, and that unruly Tupperware container playing hide-and-seek behind the pickles.

Step One

Empty everything from the fridge, and put those items on the clean countertop. Yes, I mean *everything.* Every jar, can, and mysterious container of "something" you missed in the last step and that most likely has an expiration date that predates smartphones.

Once everything is out in the open, you'll get a full view of your culinary inventory, and more importantly, you'll get a chance to clean those shelves. If your shelves haven't seen an intense soap and hot water deep-clean since the eruption of Mount St. Helens, now is the perfect time to give them a good scrub. Remember, discovering the sticky residue from last year's cranberry sauce is just part of the adventure.

You've cleared the clutter from the refrigerator and given your shelves a spa day. You're doing terrific! Next up, it's time to pull everything from the pantry—all of it. Assessing all your food inventory is crucial.

Now that your kitchen countertops look like a supermarket had a serious meltdown, it's time to go full Sherlock Holmes on those expiration dates. Is there anything past its prime that you miss on the first or second go-around? Toss it. Are items nearing their end? Highlight those—they're moving to the top of the meal plan! The goal here is simple: *waste not, want not.* The last thing you want is five jars of spaghetti sauce and no pasta. Speaking of which—*group together similar items.* Put grains with grains, sauces with sauces, and canned veggies with canned fruits. Tuna, salmon, and all canned meats together, soups and stews together—you get the picture, and honestly—that oddball assortment of mismatched Tupperware? Put them somewhere they won't reproduce overnight.

With all your pantry goods on the counter, it's time to clean those shelves. They deserve the same spa treatment as the refrigerator shelves.

Next Up

Storage solutions mentioned earlier are every Type-A personality's dream. If you're not already acquainted with bins, baskets, and clear containers, allow me to introduce your new best friends. These see-through superheroes let you know, at a glance, if you're out of rice or drowning in lentils (Vertical Spice, 2024). And don't forget labels! You'll be doing a happy twirl and whirl dance when you can find the oatmeal without playing kitchen hide-and-seek. *This* is Pantry Zen.

Let's Talk Leftovers

Holidays are notorious for that post-feast fridge full of potential science experiments—I mean, leftovers. Designate a specific zone in your fridge for these beauties (My Store Admin, 2024). This way, they won't end up growing fur behind the milk, only to be discovered weeks later, looking like a scene from a horror movie.

Speaking of creative repurposing, instead of letting that extra turkey or cranberries languish, get inventive! For instance, leftover turkey can become the star of a hearty soup or a delightful sandwich. Those extra cranberries? Turn them into a scrumptious sauce or even bake them into muffins. The possibilities are endless. Repurposing food not only prevents waste but also keeps meals feeling fresh and exciting. If creativity isn't your thing, don't worry—there are plenty of websites that'll take your list of random ingredients and craft a full gourmet recipe for you. Repurposing food prevents waste and adds some fun twists to your meals.

With all your food items back in place in the clean refrigerator and pantry, with a little effort, you'll have a pantry and fridge so well organized that you'll actually enjoy cooking—or at least, you won't dread it as much. Plus, you'll avoid the ultimate kitchen nightmare: those green, hairy science experiments better suited for a high school laboratory.

Daily Maintenance Tips

Now that we've cleared the decks, how do we keep them that way? Enter a few simple daily maintenance habits—because we all love living in an oasis, not a disaster zone. One top-notch trick is the 'five-minute tidy.' Set a timer for five minutes each day, and channel your inner Flash as you zip through the kitchen like a storm, putting items back where they belong. This quick blitz keeps clutter from creeping back and turning into the towering Everest of junk you dread climbing later.

Another golden rule: ensure everything has its own home. Whether it's utensils, spices, or that one brown sock that has mysteriously decided to camp out in the junk drawer, put them back in their cozy spots after use. Consistency is the name of the game here—it helps you avoid becoming a military policeperson, searching for things like an amateur sleuth on a missing-person case. It truly helps minimize mess in the long run.

Designate Storage for Appliances

Bulky appliances often pretend they're magical wonder towers, each taking up way too much precious countertop real estate. But fear not, courageous warrior! We will introduce some clever storage solutions so you can banish those oversized offenders without sacrificing functionality. Think about shoving that bread maker you only use once a month into the pantry or tucking away that waffle iron that only sees action on pancake Sundays. Freeing up these spaces can make you feel like a kitchen magician!

Consider investing in some fabulously stylish storage solutions. Think chic shelves or cabinets that help hide big appliances while turning your kitchen into a visual paradise. Solutions like appliance garages (those adorable roll-top bins) can keep your toaster and blender accessible yet out of sight. Nobody needs to see your rice cooker lounging around like it's on a permanent vacation, especially when company is coming over!

Incorporate Decorative Elements

Just because we're decluttering doesn't mean your kitchen should feel like a sterile lab where joy goes to die. If you didn't previously, sprinkle in some decorative elements that boost the festive vibe without adding to the clutter avalanche. Maybe some seasonal flowers in a cute vase or a bowl overflowing with colorful fruits that could make even the grumpiest person smile. Perhaps a whimsical holiday-themed centerpiece that shouts, "Look at me, I'm festive!" These decor items can bring warmth and cheer to your kitchen, creating the perfect setting for those epic holiday feasts. Go wild and rotate decorations to keep things fresh! Pumpkins and gourds in the fall can be replaced by poinsettias and cranberries for the winter festivities. This approach keeps decorations lively, preventing them from becoming the kitchen version of wallpaper—stale and boring.

Maintain the Momentum

So, what happens after the initial cleaning frenzy and organizing blitz? Maintaining a clean and functional kitchen is like a marathon, not a sprint. Regularly take a peek at your kitchen's layout and make small adjustments as needed. If you find an appliance is still occupying too much space or you've mysteriously amassed more "stuff" again, don't hesitate to revisit these tips. After all, the goal is to create a kitchen environment that looks fabulous and serves you well, especially when you're knee-deep in pie crusts, cookies, and gravy boats during the holiday season!

Setting up a Baking Station for Holiday Treats

As the holidays roll in, there's nothing quite like the glorious aroma of freshly baked goodies wafting through the house. But if your kitchen resembles a disaster scene straight out of a tornado alley, it's time to establish a dedicated baking station (CoCo, 2023). This not only boosts efficiency but also adds a sprinkle of joy—like confetti for your culinary adventures.

Creating a dedicated space for baking projects can transform your holiday experience from chaos into a merry adventure. Imagine having all your baking essentials and ingredients in one spot! It's so much easier to whip up a batch of festive treats without throwing your back out searching for that elusive rolling pin. Designating a specific area for baking means less clutter and more focus on creating yummy memories, keeping the rest of your kitchen open for other culinary shenanigans.

The key to an efficient baking station is having all your tools within arm's reach. Make sure you've got the basics: measuring cups and spoons, mixing bowls, a sturdy rolling pin, and all those baking trays, pie plates, and cake pans you've accumulated over the years—because we all need at least six different sizes of cake pans, right? Store these items near the oven because most, if not all, of your baked goods will come from the oven when done. To avoid the mid-recipe quest that feels like a scavenger hunt, keep whisks, spatulas, and cookie cutters handy near the stove in drawers or clear bins in the cupboards. Having everything organized and easily accessible by the oven saves time and steps and, in the long run, minimizes frustration—especially when you're sporting a new outfit dusted in flour!

Organizing your ingredients is another crucial step. Holidays often mean baking in quantities large enough to feed a small country, which can lead to a cluttered workspace more irrepressible than a dog trying to get the squirrel just outside the window. Streamline the process by keeping frequently used ingredients together, such as flour, sugar, baking powder, baking soda, and spices. Consider investing in clear containers for these staples; they keep your ingredients fresh and let you see at a glance when you're running low. This is particularly useful for prepping cookie or cake batches ahead of time, saving you from frantic runs to the store for more sugar! It ensures that your treats are always ready for guests or gifting.

Now, let's add a dash of holiday cheer to your new baking station. Incorporating festive elements into your baking station can make the task more enjoyable and get everyone in the holiday spirit. Deck your station with holiday-themed aprons, oven mitts, and dish towels. Incorporating decorative elements into the baking station doesn't have to be a grand affair. Simple touches like a miniature Christmas tree, holiday-shaped cookie cutters, and a small jar of fresh cranberries can brighten your cooking space. A little touch of festivity goes a long way in making your baking station functional and festive. Don't forget to blast your favorite holiday tunes while you bake; it adds an extra layer of joy to the whole experience!

Utilizing storage solutions like bins, baskets, and containers can dramatically improve your organization. Labeling these beauties gives you that neat and tidy vibe and makes finding ingredients as easy as pie (pun intended), eliminating the guesswork and reducing waste.

Consider dedicating a drawer for tiny items like food coloring, sprinkles, and piping bags—we all know how easily those can disappear into the kitchen Twilight Zone! Clear storage allows for quick checks and keeps everything tidy, promoting a stress-free environment.

What's more, if you have one, turning your kitchen island into a baking hub could be a game changer. If your island sits parallel to the oven, it's the perfect spot for your baking station and to store mixing bowls, spatulas, cookie cutters, mixing spoons, baking pans, cake decorating supplies, rolling pins, and rolling mats. All items can be neatly tucked away in various containers, ranging from glass jars to metal vintage baskets. The top of the island can serve as a food prep area, and leaving your stand mixer out year-round means it's always ready when inspiration strikes. If you don't have a kitchen island, consider using a mobile workstation or kitchen cart. Place festive table mats on the shelves below for baking items and supplies. A set of cabinets can also be used to create your baking nook.

One of the best parts about having a well-organized baking station is how it enhances cleanliness and ease of access. Keeping your station close to the sink makes cleanup quicker, and proximity to the oven means you can monitor your baked goods without doing the kitchen cha-cha. This setup cuts down on unnecessary movements, helping you stay efficient and focused and, in the long run, less tired from extra unnecessary steps. After all, the only drama in the kitchen should be from the buttercream frosting showdown! This is all about creating an environment where you feel comfortable and inspired to bake.

Baking is as much about the experience as it is about the final product. Establishing a dedicated baking station sets the stage for creating delicious treats and cherished memories. Whether you're baking with family or friends or enjoying some solo time in the kitchen, a well-prepared and festive baking station makes the process smooth and delightful.

Setting up a dedicated baking station adds that extra layer of joy and efficiency, turning holiday baking into a delightful experience rather than an uninvited nightmare. Whether you're whipping up batches of cookies or turning leftovers into something fabulous, an organized kitchen is your secret weapon for a smooth and enjoyable holiday season. Embrace these tips, bake with flair, and transform your kitchen into holiday fun, laughter, and culinary creativity (Mindful Decluttering & Organizing, 2019). So, go ahead and sprinkle a little organizational magic into your kitchen. You've got this!

Chapter Summary for Busy People

- **Pantry and fridge: Expired food galore**

    - Time for a ruthless inventory—ditch expired items and food that never left the shelf. Anything fermenting? Toss it.

- **Countertops: Clear and functional**

    - Remove the clutter—gadgets, mushy fruit, random mail. Only keep what's useful for cooking or adding a festive touch.

- **Storage solutions: Your new best friends**

    - Bins, baskets, and clear containers are key. Label everything for easy access and organization. Bonus points for holiday-themed storage!

- **Leftovers: Designate a zone**

    - Keep a specific fridge area for leftovers to avoid surprise science experiments later.

- **Daily maintenance: Five-minute blitz**

    - Set a timer for five minutes of daily tidying to keep chaos at bay.

- **Appliance storage: Clear counter space**

  - Hide bulky appliances you rarely use—keep only what you need on the countertops.

- **Decor: Festive, not overboard**

  - Add holiday-themed towels or a small seasonal centerpiece, but don't turn your kitchen into Santa's workshop.

- **Baking station: Dedicated space**

  - Set up a baking station near the oven for easy access to all your tools and ingredients. Make it festive, too!

- **Repurpose leftovers: Get creative**

  - Turn leftover turkey into soup or sandwiches and extra cranberries into muffins or sauces. Minimize food waste and keep meals exciting.

- **Final tip: Keep it simple**

  - Stick with small, manageable tasks. You'll have a functional and festive kitchen ready for holiday feasts!

CHAPTER 5:

Bedroom Bliss: Create a Calm Retreat Amidst Festivities

Falling into bed after a day filled with holiday lunacy should feel like diving into a fluffy cloud of peace, not stumbling through a minefield of holiday socks, misplaced shoes, and that one scarf you swore you'd wear but never did. Let's face it—nothing ruins that cozy sanctuary vibe like tripping over clutter in the dark. But don't worry! Creating a calm, festive retreat in your bedroom amidst the holiday disorder isn't just some wild fantasy. It's totally doable with a few intentional changes, seasoned with a good dose of humor because, honestly, what's life without a bit of laughter, especially when you're knee-deep in the laundry?

Imagine this: You walk into your room and *gasp*—everything is where it should be! Your favorite sweater isn't hiding under a mountain of random clothes, your bedside table no longer looks like a small convenience store, and you can actually find your bed without needing a treasure map. Sounds like a dream, right? Well, buckle up because we're about to make that dream a reality—*before* your holiday pie gets cold.

This chapter will tackle your wardrobe and show you how to sort through your clothes without turning your bedroom into the set of "Stockpiling Gone Biserk." Trust me; you don't need to keep every regrettable 90s fashion choice (yes, I'm talking about those neon hammer pants—let them go, my friend). It's all about figuring out what sparks joy and what needs to be released into the universe like the fashion faux pas it is.

And let's not forget about that bedside table. Honestly, who really needs seven half-empty water bottles, three mismatched socks, and a stack of unread magazines plotting a coup against your sleep space? Not you! We'll help you clear that mess out so your bedside can finally look like a place where you actually want to rest rather than a disaster zone in waiting.

But we're not stopping there! You'll also learn how to create designated relaxation zones that make your room say "ahh" instead of "ugh." Imagine your bedroom with a touch of festive joy, where you can unwind without being ambushed by clutter because even your bedroom deserves a little holiday magic.

So, ready to dive in and reclaim your bedroom from the holiday wackiness? Let's get started before your bed starts calling for a clutter intervention!

Clear Out Wardrobe Clutter

Ah, the wardrobe – that black hole where clothes from every era, fashion disaster, and questionable sale bin seem to gather like they're hosting a secret reunion. Decluttering your wardrobe isn't just about making space; it's about freeing yourself from the clutches of that neon green sequin dress you *swore* would come back into style but only makes you look like a disco ball fell into a vat of radioactive waste. And trust me, when the holidays hit, and you're trying to find something that screams "festive chic" rather than "I just woke up," you'll thank yourself for the clean-out.

Let's explore how to declutter your wardrobe while adding humor (and probably some tears) along the way. Also, don't worry—I'll sprinkle those expert quotes and sources throughout—because if you're going to suffer through a wardrobe purge, at least do it with academic backing!

Step 1: The Great Clothes Avalanche—Assessing What You Own

Imagine this: You walk into your closet, fully intending to "take a quick peek," and suddenly, an avalanche of forgotten clothing tumbles out like it's auditioning for a B-grade disaster movie. If your floor is buried under mismatched socks, jeans that haven't seen daylight since high school, and scarves that multiply like they're running a secret textile factory, it's time to *deal*.

The method: Start by pulling everything out of your closet. Yes, everything. I know. It feels like you're betraying your own sanity, but this is necessary. How else will you rediscover that suede fringe jacket hiding behind a pile of "aspirational size" pants?

Once you have everything laid out and perhaps feel an overwhelming urge to sob, take a deep breath and channel your inner decluttering freedom fighter. As you go through each item, ask yourself these questions:

- Do I remember buying this?

- Have I worn it in the past year?

- Does it still fit, or do I need to lie to myself about this fact?

- Does it spark joy, or does it spark the need to apologize to my closet?

Holly Aiello (2023) suggests asking these kinds of questions to give your brain a much-needed break from decision fatigue. Questions will reduce the mental gymnastics of figuring out if that sweater you shrunk in the wash might still work as a crop top for someone a third your size. Spoiler alert: It won't.

Step 2: Bid Farewell, Fashion Faux Pas

Now, let's get ruthless. We all have those fashion missteps we'd rather forget—the leopard print leggings you bought in a misguided 3 a.m. online shopping spree, or that cardigan that looked "kind of cool" until you realized it's more "school librarian chic" than anything else. If an item hasn't graced your body in a year, it's time to say goodbye.

There are three paths for these former "fashion friends:" donation, upcycling, or the trash heap. Aiello (2023) is all about spreading holiday cheer through donations and recommends you send those still-serviceable clothes to a nursing home, church, or local charity. What better way to celebrate the season of giving than to pass along that paisley blouse to someone else who has no idea what they're in for?

But don't be afraid to throw away items that are beyond hope. That pair of jeans with the rip in the back pocket isn't going to resurrect itself, no matter how hard you try. And don't even *think* about giving those to charity unless you want the donation bin folks to nominate you for "Worst Dressed Ghost of Christmas Past."

Step 3: The Great Seasonal Switcheroo

Congratulations—you've survived the first two rounds! But before you get too smug and call it a day, it's time to tackle the next hurdle: rotate your wardrobe by season. Unless you plan to wear your beloved summer crop tops in the middle of a snowstorm, you don't need everything at once.

Pack away sundresses, beachwear, strappy sandals and summer shoes using vacuum-sealed bags or storage bins. These take up less space and give you the satisfaction of watching your clothes shrink like a bad laundry mishap (this time, it's intentional). Once you've sealed up the out-of-season items, store them in a way that won't make you hate your life when spring rolls around and you have to find them again.

According to Orgadmin (2023), using seasonal storage helps prevent the feeling that your closet is a claustrophobic nightmare. The next time you open your wardrobe, you won't be fighting off sundresses when you're reaching for a woolly sweater. It's like packing away the ghosts of seasons past—minus the whole creepy Victorian vibe.

Step 4: Hanger Games—May the Odds Be Ever in Your Closet's Favor

Speaking of woolly sweaters, let's take a moment to talk about hangers. Yes, hangers. Those underappreciated skeletons of closet organization can be the difference between your wardrobe looking sleek and chic or like a laundry room up-chucked.

Pro tip: Invest in some high-quality, matching hangers. I know what you're thinking: "Does it *really* matter?" Oh, it does. Nothing screams "I've got my life together" more than a row of matching velvet hangers. You might not have your life together, but your closet can sure as heck fake it. Velvet hangers, in particular, are great because they prevent your clothes from slipping off like they're fleeing the *Titanic.*

If you really want to take it up a notch, color-code your hangers by season. Aiello (2023) recommends using yellow for summer, orange for autumn, red for winter, and blue for spring. This way, when you're half-asleep and trying to find something to wear, you'll at least know you've grabbed the right season. It's not foolproof (we can't help if you've accidentally paired your summer flip-flops with winter wool pants), but it's a step in the right direction.

Step 5: Decluttering Like a Pro—Or, at Least, a Pretend Pro

Now, just when you think you're done, enter the idea of a *continual* decluttering system. Set up a donation bin right in your closet or bedroom. Whenever you try on something that doesn't fit or doesn't make you feel like a budding superstar, toss it into the bin. Over time, you'll develop the habit of getting rid of clothes that no longer serve you, like an ex who "forgot" to text back.

Poplin (Dickson, 2023) encourages people to stay vigilant about clutter creep. She argues that decluttering isn't a one-time affair—it's more like a yearly wardrobe confession. Keep the donation bin handy, and you'll never again face an overwhelming purge right before the holidays (when your patience is already running thin).

Step 6: Side Tables Aren't Just for Dust Collecting Anymore

With the closet in a state of Zen-like calm, let's talk about bedside tables. These innocent little pieces of furniture are deceptive, aren't they? One day, you have a simple lamp and book on them; the next, you've got enough clutter to open a small general store. I mean, how many tubes of lip balm does one person actually need within arm's reach?

Julianna Poplin (Dickson, 2023) insists that your nightstand is prime real estate for serenity. Before bed and after waking up, it's often the first and last thing you see, and the last thing you need before trying to sleep is a reminder of that pile of unpaid bills or last month's grocery list.

Start by clearing off everything except the essentials. Lamp? Yes. Book? Absolutely. Half-empty coffee mug from three days ago? Nope, off to the kitchen with that. As for the miscellaneous items like reading glasses, phone chargers, and those eight bottles of lotion—tuck them into the drawers—bottom drawer if possible. If your bedside table doesn't have drawers, it's time to upgrade, my friend. We're talking multifunctional storage like it's your new best friend.

My bedside table has two drawers. The top drawer holds a complete set of undergarments for the week. By set, I mean socks, underwear—you get it—the works. During arctic cold mornings, I want those items close by after climbing out of a warm, toasty bed—very close!

Prerna Jain (Dickson, 2023) recommends drawer dividers for maximum efficiency. By giving everything its own little home inside your drawer, you can avoid digging through everything when you need something simple. It's like organizing a mini world of nighttime necessities—without needing a search-and-rescue team whenever you need your phone charger.

Declutter the Bedroom Chest of Drawers: A Comedy of Socks and Surprises

Ah, the bedroom chest of drawers. The unsung hero of your room—or perhaps more accurately, the black hole of odd socks, tangled jewelry, and clothes that somehow shrink after every wash. If your drawers have become more of a game of Tetris than a place of calm and order, it's time to declutter and organize. Don't worry; it's not as terrifying as finding that one arrogant spider who definitely had a plan to make a winter home in your chest of drawers.

Step 1: The Drawer Dump

First things first: dump everything out. Yes, that's right, everything. No half measures here. We're going full "I'm about to change my life" mode. Just be prepared for what you might find in there—because, let's be honest, if you dig deep enough, you'll probably unearth relics of your past. That's right, there's that ticket stub from a concert you swear you threw away, and hey, maybe you'll find the missing sock that's been playing hide-and-seek for years.

As professional organizer Julie Morgenstern advises, sometimes the best way to start decluttering is to "create a fresh slate" by clearing everything out. It's like pressing reset, minus the annoying tech jargon. Plus, seeing everything spread out will help you decide what really belongs in those drawers and what needs to go.

Step 2: The Great Sort (or Confronting Your Sock Situation)

Now, you've got a mountain of stuff that might make Everest look tiny; start sorting—shirts with shirts, socks with socks, and whatever that mystery object is with "things you'll deal with later" (just don't let "later" be five years from now).

And socks. Oh, the socks. How do we end up with so many mismatched pairs? At this point, they're leading their own double lives.

If you're holding onto a lonely sock waiting for its mate to return from wherever lost socks go—perhaps an unknown hidden underground bunker—it's time to let it go. The National Association of Productivity & Organizing Professionals (NAPO) recommends tackling small categories one at a time—like your sock collection—so you don't get overwhelmed. Start small; you'll be a decluttering warrior before you know it.

Step 3: The "Do I Really Need This?" Game

As you go through your collection of clothes and random items, it's time to play a fun little game called "Do I Really Need This?" This game involves you getting brutally honest with yourself. Do you know that shirt you've been holding for years, waiting for the perfect occasion that never comes? Spoiler alert: the occasion isn't coming. If you haven't worn it in a year, it's time to part ways. Professional organizer Peter Walsh often asks his clients to ask themselves, "Would I buy this again today?" If the answer is no, it's probably time to say goodbye.

If something hasn't sparked joy since 2008, it's safe to say it's time to toss, donate, or re-gift it (your secret is safe with me).

Step 4: Organize Like You Mean It

Now that you've cleared the clutter, let's get to the fun part—organizing! Organizing is where you get to make your drawers the envy of Instagram. First off, invest in some drawer dividers or boxes. Yes, I'm asking you to embrace order. Without them, your carefully organized drawers will return to a mess faster than you can say, "I just had this tidy!"

Marie Kondo, queen of the "KonMari" method, is a huge advocate for drawer dividers and boxes. By giving everything a specific home within your drawers, you're less likely to throw things in randomly, which will keep the clutter at bay. Keep everyday essentials like socks and underwear in the top drawer of your chest of drawers—or try the C

Davert method and put a few complete underwear sets in your bedside top drawer for easy access. Middle drawers are perfect for T-shirts or gym wear, while bottom drawers can house heavier or less frequently used items. It's like assigning seating at a dinner party; only this time no one will argue over who gets the best spot.

Step 5: The Folding Wars

Now, when it comes to folding, there are two types of people: the neat folders and the "I'll just shove it in and hope the drawer closes" folks. If you're in the latter group, this is your intervention.

Marie Kondo also recommends folding clothes into small rectangles and placing them upright in the drawer. This saves space and makes it easier to see everything without digging through the entire pile. Rolling your clothes instead of folding is another space-saving trick endorsed by professional organizers like Ashley Murphy and Molly Graves from NEAT Method. It'll make your drawers look like something out of an organizing magazine, even if that's the only thing in your house under control.

Step 6: Maintain the Order

Lastly, the real trick to an organized chest of drawers isn't the initial decluttering—it's keeping it that way. You'll feel all Zen for about a week before the old habits try to sneak back in. Here's a pro tip from NAPO: If tempted to shove something into the wrong drawer "just for now," remember that "just for now" becomes "forever" if you don't stop it. Do a quick check every few weeks, toss what's unnecessary, and revel in your newfound drawer mastery.

And there you have it! Your chest of drawers is no longer a mystery labyrinth but a well-oiled machine of organized bliss. Now, you can find that favorite shirt without climbing Mount Miscellaneous or consulting a map.

So go ahead and open those drawers with pride. And if you find a few more mismatched socks, just know there's probably an alternate dimension out there chock full of them.

Step 7: The Reading Nook You Deserve

Once you've tackled the wardrobe and bedside table, it's time to create a little sanctuary within your bedroom: the reading nook. Now, you don't need a massive space for this—just a cozy corner with a comfy chair, a warm blanket, and maybe a few decorative pillows. Think "cozy retreat," not "makeshift landfill."

A well-lit nook, with a soft lamp and some good reads, can become your haven from the holiday havoc. Lauren (2023) insists that creating these serene zones is crucial for surviving the end-of-year nonsense. You'll thank yourself when you escape to your nook with a cup of tea while the rest of the house descends into seasonal pandemonium.

Step 8: Sensory Overload—In the Good Way

Nothing says relaxation, like the perfect scent to waft you away into a land of calm. Lavender, chamomile, vanilla—pick your aromatherapy weapon of choice. Adding a few scented candles or a diffuser to your bedroom is a simple yet transformative trick for your mood and space. According to Lorie Marrero (2023), fragrances can create a subconscious connection to peaceful moments, so when you smell them, your mind can be tricked into winding down, no matter how absurd the day has been.

Just be cautious not to go overboard. This area isn't a perfume shop; it's your bedroom. Aim for subtlety—no one wants their space to smell like they've been trapped inside a bath bomb factory. A gentle, calming aroma can help you sleep better, which is exactly what we all need when the holiday stress starts to mount.

Step 9: Sentimental Items—AKA the "How Can I Get Rid of This?" Dilemma

Ah, sentimental items—the Achilles' heel of decluttering. Old love letters, the t-shirt from your first concert, or that knit sweater your great aunt made you in 1998 that hasn't fit in a decade or two. We hold onto these things not because they're particularly useful but because they tug at our heartstrings. The problem is that they also take up space—precious space.

Here's a compromise: Instead of holding onto every little knickknack and piece of memorabilia, pick a few select items that genuinely evoke positive memories that you can display or store properly. Marie Kondo (2019), the queen of decluttering, suggests keeping only those sentimental items that "spark joy." Keep it if it makes you smile or gives you a happy feeling. If it reminds you of a weird phase in college, maybe it's time to let it go.

Consider creating a memory box for the sentimental items you can't part with but don't want to display. Store it neatly, and only open it on special occasions when you're ready to take a trip down memory lane. Prerna Jain (2023) suggests limiting sentimental collections to one box per person to avoid hoarding under the guise of nostalgia.

Step 10: Maintenance—Your New Best Friend

By now, your wardrobe and entire bedroom should look fresh, organized, and totally functional. The trick, though, is keeping it that way. We all know how easy it is to fall back into old habits—clothes strewn on the floor or shoes piling up in a corner comparable to an NFL football huddle. So, how do you keep the clutter from creeping back?

First, make it a point to revisit your wardrobe and bedroom organization every few months. Seasonal changes are the perfect excuse to do a mini-clean. As you rotate your clothes, assess whether anything needs to be donated or tossed. According to Holly Aiello

(2023), doing these minor touch-ups regularly prevents the overwhelming feeling of a total closet catastrophe.

Second, embrace the "one in, one out" rule. Every time you buy something new—whether it's clothes, shoes, or decor—get rid of something old. This keeps your closet and living space from becoming cluttered again. And really, do you *need* another black sweater? Spoiler alert: You probably already have five.

Lastly, set up regular donation days. Every six months or every year, you take a bag of clothes or unused items to a local charity. Not only will you maintain a clutter-free home, but you'll be helping others in the process. Aiello (2023) mentions that decluttering with a purpose makes the whole process feel more meaningful, turning what could be a mundane task into a small act of kindness.

Chapter Summary for Busy People

- **Prioritize peace**
  - Your bedroom should be a cozy retreat, not a cluttered disaster.
  - Avoid stumbling over holiday chaos; make it your haven!
- **Declutter your wardrobe**
- **Assess everything**
  - Take everything out of your closet.
  - Ask yourself: *Do I remember buying this? Have I worn it in the last year?*
- **Let go of unused items**
  - If you haven't worn it in a year, it's time to say goodbye.
  - Use three paths: donate, upcycle, or trash.

- **Seasonal switcheroo**

  - Pack away off-season clothes to make room for what you need now.

- **Optimize your hangers**

  - Matching hangers make your closet look organized.

  - Consider color-coding by season for easy access.

- **Continuous decluttering**

  - Keep a donation bin handy.

  - Toss items that don't fit or spark joy as you go, avoiding a last-minute holiday purge.

- **Simplify your nightstand**

  - Clear unnecessary items. Essentials only: lamp, book, and maybe a glass of water.

  - Use drawer dividers for organization.

- **Organize your chest of drawers**

  - **Start with a clean slate:** Empty your drawers completely to take inventory.

  - **Sort by category:** Group items by type (e.g., socks, shirts) to see how much you own.

  - **Purge ruthlessly:** Use the "one-year rule" (haven't worn it in a year? Let it go). Donate, recycle, or toss items that don't spark joy.

  - **Organize with purpose:** Use dividers, small boxes, or trays to keep items separate and easy to find.

  - **Utilize prime real estate:** Place frequently used items in top drawers and lesser-used items in bottom ones.

  - **Maintain it:** Schedule regular check-ins to ensure the system stays intact (e.g., monthly mini-declutters).

- **Incorporate expert tips**
    - Julie Morgenstern emphasizes organizing from the inside out.
    - Peter Walsh advocates for emotional decluttering.
    - NEAT Method's Ashley Murphy and Molly Graves focus on functional and stylish organization.
    - **Make it fun**: Inject humor and personal touches to enjoy the process—turn decluttering into a game or challenge with family.
- **Create a cozy reading nook**
    - Set up a small corner with a comfy chair, a warm blanket, and good books for a relaxing escape.
- **Incorporate calming scents**
    - Use subtle fragrances like lavender or vanilla to create a relaxing atmosphere—no overpowering smells!
- **Handle sentimental items**
    - Keep only a few meaningful mementos.
    - Consider a memory box for items you can't display but still want to keep.
- **Establish a maintenance routine**
    - Regularly revisit your organization.
    - Every few months, do a quick clean-up and embrace the "one in, one out" rule.
- **Schedule regular donations**
    - Plan donation days every six months to maintain a clutter-free space while helping others.

CHAPTER 6:

Efficiently Decluttering Bathrooms: Spa-Like Serenity

Welcome to the Bathroom Battlefield, where toothpaste tubes go to die, soap bars mysteriously vanish, and you haven't seen the bottom of that drawer since the Obama administration. We are going deep under the sink, exploring an area that makes landfills look like national parks. Everything disappears into this abyss. Cleaning supplies? Gone. Backup toilet paper? Missing in action. Maybe a cat got lost down there, too—who knows?

Today, we're decluttering your bathroom. And we're not just talking about organizing it—we're giving it a full-blown makeover. The goal? A peaceful, spa-like sanctuary where you can escape the whirlwind of life for a glorious 15 minutes a day. Let's jump in and make this dream a reality and create that little slice of heaven—before reality catches up and you have to deal with whatever fresh foolishness awaits.

Confront Your Product Stash

That seaweed face mask? Is it starting to smell less refreshing ocean breeze and more dead fish at low tide? Does that fancy serum have the consistency of runny yogurt? You're about to embark on a heroic journey of saying goodbye to products that have either:

Expired (they deserve a peaceful end).

Failed to deliver on their magical promises (curse you, voluminous shampoo that made me look like a wet Goldendoodle).

If it's crusty, slimy, or gives off a scent that would make your dog whimper, toss it. Trust me, your bathroom will smell less like chemical Eau de parfum and more like the aromatherapy commercial you once dreamed it could be.

Step 1: Pull everything out. Again, I said *everything*. That includes the weird off-brand conditioner that smells like disappointment and the tube of lipstick that you swore would be your signature color but instead makes you look like a retired clown. Pile it all up like you're creating a mountain of guilt—one that you'll soon be free from.

Sort, Toss, and Mourn Your Expired Products

Now that your bathroom looks like an apocalyptic wasteland of forgotten beauty products, it's time for the second step: *the purge*. It's time to ask some tough questions. Start with the basics:

- Is this product expired? (If you don't know, just assume yes—if it smells like chemical warfare, toss it.)

- Have I used this in the past six months? If the answer is no, say goodbye.

- Does this bring me joy, or does it bring me confusion and slight nausea?

According to *Dr. Holly Aiello* (2023), expired cosmetics can cause skin irritation, clogged pores, and overall bad juju. Do you really want to risk that over a 4-year-old mascara that's somehow turned into a brittle stick of sadness? I didn't think so.

Here's a tip: If your product labels have faded to the point where you can't tell what it is anymore, that's a solid clue that it's time to let it go. And remember, just because you spent money on it doesn't mean you're contractually obligated to keep it forever. Think of it this way: eliminating it frees up space for new, *non-expired* purchases (Aiello, 2023).

Organize Like You're in a Pinterest Fever Dream

Now that your bathroom floor has trash bags full of expired beauty products no longer needed, you're probably feeling lighter, happier, and maybe a little bit emotionally drained. That's normal. Decluttering is hard work, both physically and emotionally. But fear not—the fun part is about to begin: organization.

Here's the deal: you don't need to create a full-blown minimalist shrine to cleanliness, but you do need to implement some basic organizational strategies so you don't end up right back where you started (you know—messy mess). The key is to think like an overly ambitious Pinterest user, one who's ready to color-code their life into oblivion.

Containers, Containers, Containers!

If you don't have a drawer full of tiny baskets and jars by the end of this, you've done it wrong. We're talking baskets for under the sink, trays for countertops, and drawer dividers that will make you feel like you've got your life together (even if you don't). The idea here is to give every item a home. If it doesn't have a home, then *it doesn't belong* (Lauren, 2023).

> **Pro tip:** Label your baskets. This might seem over-the-top, but trust me, when you're searching for a band-aid in a moment of crisis, you'll be so happy you labeled them.

Toilet Paper Towers: Making Storage Sexy Again

Ah, the eternal struggle: where to store the toilet paper. You want it accessible but don't want it to look like you're prepping for a toilet paper apocalypse. Luckily, there's a middle ground between storing it on the back of the toilet (tacky) and hiding it in a closet three rooms away (impractical).

Consider stackable bins or floating shelves to create a visually appealing *toilet paper tower* (Jain, 2023). I know what you're thinking—how could toilet paper ever be sexy? But trust me, with the right shelves and a touch of creativity, you'll have your toilet paper looking like a modern art installation in no time.

The "Medicine Cabinet of Doom": Tackle the Over-the-Sink Disaster Zone

If your medicine cabinet looks like a pharmaceutical company took up residency inside it, you're not alone. The medicine cabinet is a notorious clutter hotspot, but it doesn't have to be. Follow these simple steps, and you'll transform it from a never-ending mess into a sleek, organized paradise.

Step 1: Purge old medications. If the bottle reads "2016" and is covered in dust, it's time to let go. Expired medications are useless and potentially dangerous. *Lauren Dickinson* (2023) insists that decluttering the medicine cabinet should be an annual event. So, say goodbye to those ancient cough syrups and mystery pills (Marrero, 2023).

Step 2: Install magnetic strips inside the cabinet door to hold tweezers, nail clippers, and other small metal items. Magnetic strips are a lifesaver for anyone who's tired of losing tweezers into the dark abyss of the medicine cabinet. Plus, they'll make you feel like a DIY genius whenever you open the door.

And here's the game-changer: cabinet door storage. That's right. Those doors can hold more than just the occasional splash of toothpaste. Hang up your hair dryer, curling iron, and maybe even your will to live (kidding…kind of).

Shower Power: Winning the War on Shampoo Bottles

Raise your hand if your shower is housing at least five half-used shampoo bottles. Yep, that's what I thought. We've all been there—buying a new shampoo before finishing the old one because *this one smells like coconuts*, and suddenly, your shower looks like a product testing lab.

Step 1: Get a caddy. No, I don't mean a golf caddy (although, if you're desperate enough, that might work too). I'm talking about a simple, elegant shower caddy that hangs on your showerhead or sticks to the wall. These will immediately reduce the bottle clutter and make your shower look 100% more organized (Poplin, 2023).

Step 2: Implement a strict one-in, one-out rule. From now on, you should only have one shampoo, one conditioner, and one body wash in your shower at a time. If you want to try a new product, you have to finish the old one first. It's like shampoo rehab, and you're going to emerge victorious.

Towel Tales: Time to Upgrade

Remember when you wrapped yourself in your favorite towel, but it felt more like being sandpapered than hugged? Yeah, it's time for an upgrade. Go ahead, grab that crumpled bare thread towel you've had since the first Bush administration, and *toss it*.

Now, let's talk fluffy towels. You deserve a little pampering. Picture it: you step out of the shower, and instead of feeling like you're drying off with a sad, thin rag, you grab a plush, cloud-like towel. Ahh, pure bliss! Suddenly, your bathroom is a five-star resort, and all you have to do is throw out some old towels with more holes than Swiss cheese.

The Aromatherapy Flex: Creating a Spa Vibe (Without Going Bankrupt)

Once your bathroom is decluttered, you'll want to make it feel as luxurious as possible—because why shouldn't you? You deserve to feel like you're walking into a high-end spa, not a public restroom. So, let's add some finishing touches to really up the *Zen* factor.

Step 1: Candles. Scented candles are the easiest way to add a spa-like serenity to your bathroom. Opt for scents like lavender, eucalyptus, or vanilla for maximum relaxation (Marrero, 2023). Plus, the warm glow will make your bathroom feel ten times more expensive than it actually is.

Step 2: Plants. That's right—plants aren't just for Instagram influencers anymore. Adding a few low-maintenance plants to your bathroom will improve air quality and give your space a fresh, calming vibe. If you don't have a green thumb, go for fake plants—no one has to know.

Maintenance Mode: How to Keep Your Bathroom From Turning Back Into a Dumpster Retreat

Congratulations! Your bathroom is officially a serene, organized oasis. But here's the hard part: keeping it that way. Don't worry, I've got your back.

Step 1: Set a monthly reminder to do a quick bathroom declutter. Take five minutes to check for expired products, reorganize your shelves, and make sure nothing is creeping back into "Whoa" territory (Aiello, 2023).

Step 2: Implement a daily reset. At the end of each day, take two minutes to put everything back in its place. It's a small habit but will make a huge difference in keeping your bathroom Zen-like and clutter-free.

Chapter Summary for Busy People

- **Assess the chaos:** Open the cabinet and survey the mess. Identify expired products and items you no longer use.

- **Sort and categorize**
    - Group items (e.g., skincare, haircare, cleaning supplies).
    - Keep frequently used items at eye level.

- **Maximize space**
    - Use bins or baskets to organize items.
    - Utilize vertical space with tiered organizers.

- **Hang it up**
    - Use hooks on the cabinet doors for items like towels and cleaning tools.

- **Label everything**
    - A label maker will help to identify the contents of bins.

- **Create a spa-like environment**
    - Add essential oils or scented candles for a relaxing aroma.
    - Use soft, fluffy towels and rugs for comfort.

- **Personal touches**
    - Incorporate plants and decor that inspire you.

- **Minimalism is key**
    - Choose a few pieces you love instead of cluttering surfaces.

- **Maintain order**
    - Set a weekly touch-up routine and monthly reviews.
    - Involve family members in maintaining the organization.

- **Keep it fun**
    - Embrace humor during decluttering; make it a game!

- **Enjoy your space**
    - Bask in your organized oasis and let the stress melt away.

CHAPTER 7

Minimalist Holiday Decorating: How to Keep Your Sanity and Still Feel Festive

Alright, holiday warriors—before you reach for that box of tangled lights and a peppermint mocha to "calm your nerves," let's rethink this whole holiday decorating madness. You don't need to recreate the Rockefeller Center in your living room to feel festive. This guide is here to prevent you from turning your home into a festive flea market and will help you embrace the art of "less is more." No one has time for a decor disaster when there's family drama and fruitcake debates, and outside, the inflatable snowman is once again staging an escape like it's auditioning for a role in "Snowman on the Run."

This chapter has tips on picking decorations that are as versatile as your Aunt Edna's multi-colored Jell-O salad at a family reunion. You'll learn to master the magic of neutral decorations, functional decor items, and DIY hacks that keep things stunning without the stress. We'll help you become a holiday-storage superpower to avoid a future showdown with your tangled lights. Let's transform your home into a peaceful holiday haven—without the clutter, the mess, or the credit card bill that makes you weep.

We're here to sprinkle a bit of minimalist holiday magic into your life. That means less clutter, fewer headaches, and more time to focus on what's truly important during the holiday season—like binge-watching cheesy holiday movies or consuming your body weight in festive goodies. So grab your fluffiest socks and your favorite mug of something warm and possibly spiked, and let's take a stroll down the minimalist decorating lane, where "less is more" and your sanity stays intact.

Step One: Accept You're Not a Tinsel Titan

Look, some people were born to deck the halls with boughs of holly, and those homes are basically magazine covers in December. I'm going out on a limb, and I guess you're probably not one of them. And that's okay! *Cue a deep breath.* Minimalist holiday decorating starts with accepting that your place won't (and shouldn't) look like Santa's entire workshop lives in your home. In fact, it's better this way.

Take a page from **Dolorese Mukisa's** minimalist Easter tablescape—if neutral tones and a few well-placed items can work for a spring holiday, they can work for Christmas, too! You don't need glitter raining down on every surface. No one's giving you a medal for hanging 3,000 ornaments; your cat certainly doesn't appreciate the effort. Embrace simplicity and channel your inner Zen master as you arrange a few pinecones in a tasteful bowl and call it a day.

Minimalist Tree Decor: Less Is More (And Less Equals Fewer Injuries)

Ah, the Christmas tree—the granddaddy of holiday decor. But does it really need to look like an explosion at an ornament factory? No. The more you put on that tree, the greater the potential for disaster, such as stepping on a fallen ornament that has shattered under the weight of your 2015 souvenir collection. Ouch.

Take it from Abby Lawson, who nails the concept of a "home uniform" in her blog. She recommends sticking to a few key colors that work with your home's overall vibe. This is the difference between your tree looking like a chic minimalist dream and resembling an overwhelmed department store display.

And let's talk ornaments. I know you love those sentimental DIY ornaments your kids made, but maybe tuck the macaroni art a little farther back this year—your guests don't need to know about it unless they're *really* into abstract art. The goal here is elegance without excess, sparkle without stress, and fewer moments where you wonder if untangling the lights qualifies as an upper-body workout.

The Wondrous Wreath: A Low-Effort, High-Impact Masterpiece

Let's hear it for wreaths! If decorating your entire home feels overwhelming, the wreath is your new best friend. It says, "I tried," without really trying at all. You can slap one of these beauties on your front door, hang it over your fireplace, or toss it on your coffee table as a centerpiece, and boom—you're officially festive.

Heidi S. from Eleanor Rose Home knows the power of simplicity, advocating for wreaths made from natural greenery with a touch of understated charm. A wreath doesn't have to scream holiday cheer at the top of its lungs; it just needs to whisper it. Bonus points if you use real evergreens—because when January rolls around, you can compost that bad boy instead of awkwardly cramming it into a box labeled "Wreaths and Things I Regret."

Outdoor Lights: You're a Holiday Ninja, Not a Lighthouse

Outdoor lights are fantastic—until you find yourself in a tangle of wires, thinking, *Wasn't this supposed to be fun?* You don't need to turn your house into a glowing tribute to the Northern Lights. Trust me, your wallet will thank you.

Instead of wrapping every square inch of your home in twinkling lights like a holiday burrito, take a note from Wang W. at F&J Outdoors, who preaches the gospel of "strategic placement." Less is more, people. Outline a few windows, frame the door, and toss some lights on a tree if you're feeling particularly festive. Voila! You're a holiday ninja, stealthily festive without overdoing it.

> **Pro-tip:** LED lights are energy-efficient and come in softer hues that won't make your house visible from space. NASA doesn't need to track your holiday spirit.

Personal Touches: When in Doubt, Go Sentimental (Not Sentimentally Overboard)

Remember that time you saw someone's house on Instagram, and it looked like Christmas threw up everywhere? Yeah, we're not doing that. Minimalism is about celebrating the things that truly matter—and guess what? That doesn't include 50-throw pillows with Santa's face on them.

Instead, dig into your sentimental stash and pull out the decorations that actually mean something. Dolorese Mukisa nailed it with her Easter setup, and the same principles apply here: focus on items that evoke memories and feelings, not just trends. A few well-placed family photos in holiday-themed frames, a homemade garland strung along the mantel, or even those heirloom ornaments passed down from grandma (the ones that don't look like craft disasters) will give your space a heartfelt touch without overwhelming it.

And the best part? It's totally doable without needing an entire storage unit for your seasonal swag. Plus, sentimental decorations mean fewer things to pack away later. You're welcome.

Eco-Friendly Elegance: Saving the Planet, One Holiday at a Time

Let's discuss the elephant in the room: holiday decor can be wasteful. All that plastic, glitter, and shiny stuff don't exactly scream "eco-friendly." Luckily, there's a way to make your space festive without Mother Earth giving you the side-eye.

Taya Wright offers fantastic advice in her guide to eco-friendly elegance—think natural materials like wood, greenery, and beeswax candles. If you want to step it up a notch, consider wrapping gifts in reusable fabric wraps (Google "furoshiki" for some serious wrapping inspiration). Not only will your home look like a sustainable winter wonderland, but you'll also get the satisfaction of knowing you're saving the planet; at the same time, everyone else is busy tossing out single-use wrapping paper.

And nothing says minimalist chic like natural textures. A wooden advent calendar, some fresh pine boughs, and a few handmade ornaments from recycled materials will make your home festive *and* environmentally conscious. Plus, you can sip your hot cocoa with a smug smile as your neighbors unpack their inflatable reindeer for the 10th year in a row.

Decluttering After the Holidays: Say Goodbye to Holiday Hysteria

We've all been there—January rolls around, and suddenly, you're staring at a mountain of decorations you now need to pack away. It's like a depressing game of Tetris, except you're playing with fragile ornaments and miles of tangled ribbon.

But this year, you're ready. US Keter has top-notch tips for keeping your holiday decor organized and easy to store. The first rule of post-holiday life is to label everything. Yes, it sounds tedious, but you'll be happy when you're not digging through boxes labeled "Miscellaneous Holiday Stuff" next December.

Again, invest in clear storage bins and divide things by category—ornaments in one bin, lights in another, wreaths in their own space. And here's the real secret: *wind up your lights carefully*. No one enjoys unraveling what looks like a holiday-themed octopus come January, so do yourself a favor and wrap those bad boys neatly.

Wrapping Presents: The Art of Looking Like You Put in Effort

Gift wrapping is like the final boss of holiday decorating. You want it to look thoughtful and chic, *not* like your toddler helped and not like you're trying out for "Gift Wrapping with the Stars."

Here's the minimalist trick: kraft paper and twine. Yep, that's it. Channel your inner rustic-chic guru and stick to neutral tones with simple, elegant touches. It looks amazing, but you'll also avoid the glitter mess that follows traditional wrapping paper. Plus, Wang W. reminds us that minimalist decor doesn't just apply to your home—it extends to your presents. By sticking to this easy-to-execute formula, you'll spend less time in the "wrapping dungeon" and more time drinking hot cocoa with marshmallows.

Final Thoughts: Minimalist Decorating, Maximum Cheer

Let's sum this up: holiday decorating doesn't need to be a full-contact sport. This year, keep it simple, chic, and most importantly, keep your sanity intact. From a minimalist tree to sentimental touches, you'll create a festive atmosphere that radiates warmth, charm, and, yes, holiday cheer—without requiring an army of elves to clean it up come January.

Remember: you're a holiday hero, and minimalism is your superpower. So, decorate with intention, humor, and just the right amount of sparkle. And if anyone asks why your house isn't lit up like a Vegas casino, smile and say, "It's called *restraint,* Sweetheart." They'll either nod in impressed silence or frantically Google "minimalist holiday chic" while hiding their inflatable snowman in shame.

Minimalist decorating is not just about less stuff—it's about more of the good stuff: more peace, more laughter, and more time to actually *enjoy* the holidays. So kick back, relax, and revel in the cozy, clutter-free festive vibes you've created.

Bonus Section: Tips From the Minimalist Masters

In case you need a few more gems to help you through the holiday madness, we've gathered wisdom from the decorating greats—those who have mastered the art of festive minimalism so you don't have to:

- **Dolorese Mukisa** recommends sticking to neutral colors and simple, natural elements. It's like giving your home a holiday hug without choking it with glitter.

- **Abby Lawson** suggests creating a cohesive color scheme throughout your home. This way, your decorations don't scream, "We ran out of ideas and threw in everything, including the kitchen sink."

- **US Keter** reminds us to organize our holiday decor like pros. No more frantically shoving decorations into random boxes. This year, your storage will be as serene as your new minimalist approach to life.

- **Wang W.** highlights the beauty of easy-to-store decor. If you can fit your holiday cheer into a single box without it exploding like a tinsel bomb, you're winning.

So, as you sit back with your spiked eggnog in one hand and a candy cane in the other, remember: this year, you've taken a big step toward festive sanity. Less stuff, fewer headaches, and more joy. Because that's what the holidays are really about—joy, laughter, and not having to wrestle an inflatable Santa off your roof come February.

Now, go forth and spread that minimalist holiday cheer!

And there you have it: the ultimate, lighthearted guide to minimalist holiday decorating that's perfect for everyone—no matter your style, taste, or tolerance for glitter. This year, let's ditch the stress and embrace the simplicity of less is more, all while keeping our sanity (and our homes) intact. By focusing on a minimalist approach, you can create a beautiful, stress-free holiday environment that prioritizes your sanity, your time, and—of course—your cookies.

Chapter Summary for Busy People

- **Embrace the "less is more" mentality**
    - Aim for cozy and stylish, not over-the-top. Your home doesn't need to look like a Hallmark movie set.
    - Focus on creating a warm atmosphere with fewer decorations to save time, money, and effort.

- **Start with realistic expectations**
    - Perfection is overrated—accept that your decor won't look like a magazine spread, and that's perfectly okay.
    - Embrace simplicity and avoid stressing over trying to impress others.

- **Minimalist tree: Fewer ornaments, more harmony**
    - Use a few key colors that match your home's decor (Abby Lawson's "Whole House Uniform" concept).
    - Incorporate natural textures and subtle elements— fewer ornaments mean fewer accidents!
    - Sentimental ornaments? Display them tastefully, but maybe keep the "macaroni angels" hidden in the back.

- **Wreaths: Low-effort, high-impact decor**
    - Place a simple wreath on doors or mantels for an easy but effective holiday touch.

- Opt for natural, compostable materials like evergreens and pinecones to be both festive and eco-friendly.

- **Outdoor lights: Go for a subtle glow**

  - Use strategically placed lights to avoid holiday overload (and avoid a "Christmas burrito" look).

  - Frame the house with a few well-placed strands of twinkling lights—easy to set up and take down!

- **Eco-friendly and sustainable choices**

  - Use natural elements like greenery and beeswax candles for decorations.

  - Skip excessive plastic and waste—opt for reusable fabric wraps for gifts (Taya Wright's eco-friendly tips).

- **Keep personal touches simple**

  - Display meaningful items like family photos and handmade garlands for a cozy, personal feel.

  - Stick to a few key decorations that tell your story without cluttering your space.

- **Decluttering after the holidays: Pack like a pro**

  - Label storage bins and neatly wind up lights to make next year's decorating easier (US Keter's advice).

  - Storing decor smartly means avoiding the January nightmare of tangled lights and misplaced ornaments.

- **Gift wrapping: Chic but simple**

  - Go for neutral, minimalist wrapping like kraft paper and twine (Wang W.'s advice)—it looks elegant and is easy to store.

  - Less clutter means fewer last-minute panics when it comes to wrapping gifts.

- **Humor is your best friend**
  - Laugh at the chaos and embrace imperfection—your holiday decor doesn't have to win awards; it just needs to make you smile.

CHAPTER 8

Manage Traditional Gifts and Gift-Wrapping Supplies

When faced with organizing gifts and wrapping supplies, there is a very thin line between a jolly holiday and the kind of chaos that makes you reconsider every life choice leading up to it. Picture a world where your wrapping paper doesn't unravel faster than a toddler hyped up on candy canes, your gift tags haven't entered a witness protection program, and the scissors? They are halfway across the house, leading their own daring escape. You're in the right place if that sounds like a holiday miracle. This chapter is all about creating that magical haven in your home where gift-wrapping becomes a breeze rather than a chore. No more tripping over paper rolls or digging through drawers to locate the tape. We'll explore why setting up a dedicated wrapping station could be just what you need to keep the chaos at bay and your spirits high.

Create a Dedicated Gift-Wrapping Station

Finding a little haven in your home where you can wrap gifts peacefully is like discovering a hidden gem that makes the holiday hustle more bearable. Choosing the right location for this wrapping station is crucial to avoid becoming a human trip hazard with random rolls of paper and mini panic attacks whenever you can't find the scissors. The aim is to streamline your gift-wrapping process and create a seamless system while actually enjoying the process of wrapping presents.

Choose the Right Location

Your gift-wrapping station doesn't need to be anything fancy. It could be a forgotten corner of the living room, the top of your washer, or even the back of a closet door—because, let's be real, you haven't seen the back of that closet since 2014 anyway. The main goal is to avoid setting up in a spot where you'll inevitably trip over a stray roll of paper or, worse, ruin it by walking all over it. This spot is a station for success, not sabotage.

Think vertically! You could transform the back of a door into a storage dream. Picture it: wrapping paper neatly hanging on hooks, ribbons lounging in organized pockets, and tape just sitting there like the cooperative little tool it's supposed to be. No more rolls of paper pretending they're log flumes every time you open a closet door. It's time to take control of the holiday craziness. If you're short on floor space, vertical storage can be a lifesaver and efficiently use otherwise wasted areas.

Essential Supplies to Include

Now that we've found the right spot, let's discuss what goes into this magical wrapping corner. You don't need an entire Home Depot aisle's worth of tools. But you *do* need sturdy, real-deal scissors, not the half-broken ones from the kitchen that turn cutting into an upper-body workout. We're wrapping gifts here, not training for a triathlon.

You'll need *tape*. Lots of tape. Clear tape for the standard jobs, double-sided tape for those "look, no tape!" moments, and maybe even some fancy washi tape for when you're feeling extra artsy. Don't forget the ribbons and bows either—they're the sprinkles on the cupcake of your gift wrap! And gift tags? They're not just there to make your gift look fancy—they ensure Aunt Florence doesn't accidentally end up with your brother's new socks.

Additionally, a few permanent markers in various colors can be handy for writing messages or labeling items. When all these tools are within arm's reach, wrapping becomes less of a chore and more of a creative outlet.

Incorporating a Work Surface

No matter how often you've told yourself otherwise, your lap is not a work surface. Wrapping gifts on a table is the adult thing to do; the key is a flat surface where you can stretch out all your wrapping supplies without looking like you're auditioning for an episode of "Survivor: Gift-Wrapping Edition."

A spacious table is invaluable for larger gifts. No more balancing acts on your lap or wrestling with oversized boxes on the living room floor. A stable, flat surface allows you to measure accurately, cut smoothly, and wrap efficiently. Plus, if you invest in a table with some storage options, like drawers or shelves, you can keep all your supplies tucked away but easily accessible.

Don't have a spare table? How about a piece of plywood that folds down from the wall like you're preparing for some high-stakes gift-wrapping mission? Think of it as the secret Batcave of holiday prep. You pop it down, wrap it like a pro, and when done, it folds up, leaving no trace behind—except for your newfound mastery of all things gift-wrap.

Personalize the Space

We're not just setting up a wrapping station; we're creating a wrapping wonderland! Don't just slap together some random supplies in a sad little corner—make it fun! Add a festive garland, throw in some cheerful motivational quotes (like, "Keep calm and find the scissors"), or toss in a holiday-scented candle. If you've got to spend hours here, it might as well smell like cinnamon and victory!

Use Storage Bins for Wrap, Ribbons, and Tags

Using various storage bins to keep wrapping supplies organized and easily accessible can be a game-changer, especially during the hectic holiday season.

First, selecting the right storage bins is essential. When picking your bins, consider the available space in your home. If you have a small closet or limited floor space, opt for compact, stackable bins that fit neatly into tight spots. Bigger bins may be more suitable for larger rooms or dedicated wrapping areas. When selecting, it's important to assess the number of wrapping supplies you have. An extensive collection of gift wrap requires more substantial storage, while a smaller assortment might only need a modest container.

> **Pro tip:** get bins with compartments. That way, your ribbons won't try to escape and start a life of their own behind the couch. Keep it simple, and group your supplies by type: paper in one bin, ribbons in another, and maybe one for those random leftover scraps you can never quite bring yourself to toss out.

Next up, categorizing supplies is crucial for maintaining an organized system. Start by sorting your materials into categories such as wrapping paper, gift bags, ribbons, bows, tags, and other embellishments. Placing similar items together in clear bins makes it easier to find what you need and helps you quickly see if any category needs replenishing. For example, if you notice you're running low on gift tags, you can add them to your shopping list before the next wrapping session. Use labels or color-coded markers to identify each category clearly. Markers and labels can be especially helpful if you involve other family members in the wrapping process. If everyone is involved, they will know exactly where to find and return each item.

Designating a bin for those "never used, but I can't throw this away" items is another pro-tip for managing waste. After a wrapping extravaganza, you'll likely have scraps of paper, partial rolls of ribbon, and other random leftovers. Instead of tossing these into some dark drawer, why not create a dedicated bin just for them? This way, you can grab your go-to supplies for ongoing projects—plus, it promotes recycling and reusing materials! Eco-friendly and budget-conscious? Yes, please!

Portable storage solutions are perfect for folks who like flexibility while wrapping gifts. Bins with handles or wheels make transporting your supplies from room to room easy. Want to wrap gifts while lounging in front of a great movie? Got it! Do you prefer to be outdoors soaking up the sun? No problem! Portable bins guarantee that your supplies are right there with you wherever you are. Let's hear of genius storage ideas from Emily Counts, a home organization guru. She centralizes everything using a large Kuggis box from IKEA with compartments for scissors, tape, and all that good stuff (Counts, 2019).

No more mess! For those big rolls of wrapping paper, consider taller containers like laundry bags or tall trash cans—they keep the rolls upright and clump-free. The Klunka Laundry Bag, for example, serves as a portable solution, even if it does need a little help standing upright. Lean it against a wall or tuck it neatly in a corner. Problem solved!

Typically, stores carry gift-wrapping storage boxes during the holiday season. These nifty boxes are the length of a roll of wrapping paper. Most have organizers in the lids for name tags, ribbons, and supplies. To wrap up (pun intended), here's how to set up your wrapping station:

- Selecting Appropriate Bins:

  Choose bins that match your collection size and available space. Stackable or compartmentalized bins boost storage efficiency.

- Categorizing Supplies:

  Divide supplies into categories like paper, bags, ribbons, and tags. Use labels or color code supplies to organize each group.

- Designating a Bin for Unused Items:

  Keep a special bin for scraps and partial rolls to minimize waste and have reusable materials at hand.

- Portable Storage Solutions:

  Opt for bins with handles or wheels to easily move your supplies wherever you wrap them, or use wrapping paper storage boxes. Most boxes have handles for easy movement.

By following these steps, you can turn potential frustration into organized bliss. No more last-minute treasure hunts for the right ribbon, just a smooth wrapping experience that makes the holidays so much more enjoyable!

Plan and Organize Gifts in Advance

Amid the holiday hustle and bustle, handling gift-wrapping supplies and presents often feels high on the stress meter. But with a little planning, you can flip this mind-blowing task into a streamlined process that saves time and allows you to bask in the holiday spirit with your loved ones. Let's explore how thinking ahead can help ease the last-minute panic!

Create a Gift List

The first step in tackling holiday gifting is developing your master gift list. Consider this your roadmap to holiday happiness! Make a list, and check it twice or three times, of everyone you plan to buy gifts for—family, friends, coworkers, and even your neighbor across the street who always brings in your trash cans when you are on vacation! Then, jot down thoughtful gift ideas for each person based on their interests. Instead of wandering aimlessly through stores or endlessly scrolling online, you'll have a game plan. Plus, a thorough list guarantees no forgotten gifts when someone gifts you something and you're left empty-handed!

Set Budget Limits

With your illustrious gift list ready, let's tackle the budget. Ah, the budgeting chat—everyone's favorite topic! But seriously, sticking to a budget is essential to avoid a post-holiday financial hangover. Set a spending limit that works for you, then break it down per person. Be realistic! The holidays shouldn't send you into credit card debt. Establishing these limits helps you prioritize your needs and focus on thoughtful gifts rather than just flashy ones. Remember, a heartfelt $10 gift can mean more than an impersonal $100 item.

Schedule Shopping Trips

You have your list and budget set; it's time to schedule your shopping trips. This part is a bit like giving your holiday errands a business plan! Allocate specific days for both online and in-store shopping. Spacing out your shopping sessions helps you avoid the last-minute frenzy when you grab whatever's on the shelves just to check items off your list. If you love the holiday mall buzz, shop early or late to skip the crowds. Do you prefer online retail therapy? Scout out sales and free shipping deals are offered around holidays. And when it comes to scheduling shopping trips, plan like you're launching a military operation. The key to avoiding mall madness is strategy.

Track Gift Purchases

Remember to track or journal your purchases as you check off those gift ideas. There's nothing worse than finding a gift hidden away after the holidays that you totally forgot about—like Aunt Marion getting two presents while you hang out with her extra gift in a closet! To avoid extra gift regret, using a simple tracking method is essential. You could use an Excel sheet, notebook, or planner to record what you bought, for whom, and where you stored it. This approach also ensures you stay on budget, as you have a clear view of what you've spent versus what you intended to. Want to take it one step further? Consider adding columns for gift status—bought, wrapped, or delivered—so you can see what's still on your to-do list with a glance. This simple tracking method eliminates those last-minute surprises, like discovering you forgot to wrap Dad's gift on Christmas Eve.

Suppose spreadsheets aren't your style; fear not! Many handy apps can help with gift tracking, reminding you of what's still outstanding and taking the weight off your shoulders. If technology isn't your idea of festive frolicking, a beautiful writing journal can help with gift tracking and works equally well. Plus, you don't have to boot up a computer to use it. Here's a shameless plug: in Amazon.com's search bar, type Cindy Ofmi for some beautiful journals/notebooks—great for gift-giving, too!

Final Thoughts

As we've journeyed through the process of setting up a dedicated gift-wrapping station, it's evident that a smidgen of planning can turn chaos into organization, readying you for a splendid holiday season. From scouting the perfect spot to stockpiling essential supplies and carving out a practical workspace, each section makes gift-wrapping blissful rather than burdensome. And hey, let's not forget to sprinkle in some personality to keep things lively! After all, a merry wrapping corner can transform even the most mundane tasks into a delightful experience.

Ultimately, setting up an organized gift-wrapping station is all about making your life easier—and maybe, just maybe, even a little fun. Whether you're claiming a corner of the living room or commandeering the back of a closet door, keeping things neat will help you sail through the holiday season without a meltdown (or a missing tape roll). You can enjoy a smooth and stress-free holiday season by organizing your supplies and planning gifts ahead! Happy wrapping!

Chapter Summary for Busy People

- **Avoid gift-wrapping chaos**

    - Prevent last-minute stress by organizing your wrapping supplies. A dedicated space helps avoid tripping over paper rolls and misplacing tools like scissors.

- **Create a gift-wrapping station**

    - Choose a designated spot: the back of a closet door, laundry room, or unused corner.

    - Maximize vertical space with hooks for paper rolls and pockets for ribbons and tape.

    - Personalize the space with festive decorations or candles to make wrapping enjoyable.

- **Essential wrapping supplies**

    - Sturdy scissors, plenty of tape (clear, double-sided, and decorative), and markers for labeling.

    - Keep gift tags and decorative ribbons handy—they add a special touch and ensure gifts go to the right people.

- **Work surface for wrapping**

    - Use a flat surface like a table or foldable board for easy measuring and wrapping.

    - No space? Use a piece of plywood that folds from the wall as a temporary workstation.

- **Organize with storage bins**

    - Use stackable, compartmentalized bins to separate paper, ribbons, and tags.

    - Have a designated bin for leftover wrapping supplies to minimize waste.

- o   Consider portable storage solutions like bins with
      handles for flexibility.

- **Plan Gifts in advance**

  - o   To avoid last-minute shopping stress, make a detailed
        gift list, noting everyone's interests.

  - o   Set a realistic budget to prevent overspending.

- **Track gift purchases**

  - o   Use a simple spreadsheet or app to track what you've
        bought, who it's for, and whether it's wrapped or
        delivered.

CHAPTER 9:

Maintain Decluttered Spaces Post-Holiday Season

Keeping your house tidy after the holiday season is like trying to bathe a cat—technically possible, but you'll probably have a few scratches and possibly lose a few limbs in the process. After weeks of festive frolicking, frantic gift-wrapping, and food prep that could easily put a royal wedding to shame, your house is no longer the cozy holiday haven it once was. It's more like Santa's workshop post-apocalypse—complete with tangled lights, half-eaten cookies, and wrapping paper reproducing in dark corners after midnight.

But don't worry, it doesn't have to stay that way. With some super-easy decluttering hacks, you can turn your home back into a peaceful sanctuary before you start hanging up next year's stockings. In this chapter, we'll cover some foolproof habits that'll help you reclaim your space and sanity without losing your cat or your will to live.

We're talking regular, bite-sized decluttering that makes cleaning feel less like shoveling snow off your roof and more like nibbling at a cupcake. We'll get into the life-saving magic of monthly deep cleans (yes, even that garage where old treadmills and forgotten ambitions go to die) and tackle the forgotten corners of your home that haven't seen daylight since last Christmas. Oh, and seasonal reviews—like little checkups for your sanity—will help you figure out if you really need 17 snow globes when you live in Arizona. And if that's not enough, you'll be reintroduced the legendary "one in, one out" policy—perfect for anyone who wants their space to stop looking like they're hosting a holiday-themed rummage sale. So pour a cup of hot tea or wine, no judgment, and let's turn your home back into the clutter-free haven it was meant to be. See "How to Declutter Your Home in 7 Simple Steps" - The Seeker Newsmagazine Cornwall.

https://theseeker.ca/2023/09/how-to-declutter-your-home-in-7-simple-steps/

Set up Regular Decluttering Routines

Picture this: Every Saturday, you set aside 20 minutes to attack one clutter zone. Just 20 minutes! That's less time than it takes to lose yourself in a TikTok rabbit hole or to convince your cat that the vacuum isn't a soul-sucking demon. Start with something small, like that coffee table in your living room that has somehow morphed into a mini-museum post-holiday disaster zone. It's as if a tornado of festive mishaps blew through, leaving behind remnants of wrapping paper, a forgotten cookie plate that's now inching nearer to a science experiment than dessert, and—oh look!—that mysterious half-eaten candy cane that seems to have taken up permanent residence inside the holiday centerpiece. It's a wonder how such a small surface can accumulate so much stuff—it's like the coffee table is hosting an after-party and forgot to invite you!

Then there are the end tables, those poor, unsuspecting pieces of furniture that are just trying to support your lifestyle but end up supporting a collection of random objects that would confuse even the most seasoned archaeologist. Along with those random objects, your end tables seem buried under a mountain of coasters—some stacked precariously, others suspiciously sticking together as if they're forming a union.

And let's talk about the remnant of holiday cheer. These decorative items were charming two weeks ago, but now they feel like unwanted guests lingering way past their welcome. Seriously, they look like they're auditioning for a reality show titled "When Christmas Goes Seriously Sad & Wrong." Once aglow with seasonal spirit, the festive candles now sit there like neglected props, slowly turning into a waxy sculpture of despair.

So, before settling in for another round of holiday movies you've already seen 17 times, take a moment to confront this post-holiday havoc. Decluttering your coffee table and end tables is like a magical quest: one moment, you're sipping coffee, and the next, you're unearthing treasures (and a few dust bunnies) from the depths of your furniture. Grab a trash bag, some gloves, and a donation box, and prepare to rescue your living room from the clutches of post-holiday madness! Tackle it for 20 minutes, and bam! You're already winning. Reward yourself with a snack, a nap, or just a smug feeling of superiority over your clutter (Tarr, n.d.).

While these weekly decluttering sessions are like a slow-and-steady nibble on your clutter cake, sometimes you've got to take a bigger bite. Enter monthly deep cleaning. Tackle one room like it owes you rent. The garage, for example. When your garage overflows with post-holiday junk and your car sits outside like it's being punished, it's time to clean up. Sort everything into "keep," "donate," and "burn with fire" piles (Lightspeed, n.d.).

And let's talk about seasonal reviews—those little check-ins where you ask yourself the tough questions: "Do I really need 14 snowmen figurines when I live in Arizona?" or "Why do I still own a full set of ice skates, despite never having skated and living nowhere near ice?"

Along with asking if something sparks joy, also ask, "Will this spark a fire if I don't get rid of it?" (Tagle, 2023).

But hey, if your sentimental attachment to that wonky reindeer candle holder is just too strong, you don't have to throw it out. Remember to create a Holiday Memory Box—a special place where all your quirky, meaningful holiday memorabilia can live out their days without being a daily tripping hazard. Boom. Clutter contained (Walsh, 2017).

Again, the holy grail of clutter control—the one-in, one-out rule. Every time you buy something new, you say farewell to something old. It's like a buy-one, get-one-free pass to a clutter-free life. Have you purchased a new sweater? Great! It's time to finally say goodbye to the one you've been holding onto since 2005, the one with the mysterious stain that's lived through three presidents. This way, your home stops looking like a department store hazard zone and starts feeling like a place where people, and cats or dogs, can actually live (zenhabits, 2008).

The Art of Rotating Seasonal Items

Let's talk about the dreaded seasonal item storage. After the holidays, your once majestic tree has become a spiky fire hazard, and your holiday decor looks like it's staging a rebellion. Think about organizing seasonal items properly before you get tempted to shove everything into the nearest closet. You'll be thankful when you're not battling a plastic wreath monster in July.

Invest in some bins, labels, and maybe a storage system that doesn't involve cramming everything into a closet and hoping for the best. Think of your storage as a fancy spa retreat for your holiday decor. Christmas lights deserve a little love, too; don't just ball them up like a pair of dirty socks (Andrea Dekker, 2024).

And please, for the love of sanity, rotate your decorations! Nothing says "seasonal confusion" like a pumpkin on your mantle in February. Swap out your holiday items with each new season—snowflakes in winter, flowers in spring, margarita glasses in summer, and probably more pumpkins in fall. This way, your home stays fresh, and you don't accidentally discover Easter eggs in November.

The one-in, one-out policy applies to holiday decor too. If you bring in a new reindeer decoration, let an old one go. Don't let your house become a shrine to last year's tacky trends (Lightspeed, n.d.).

Declutter, Don't Hoard

At some point, you'll have to face reality: you don't need every single holiday knick-knack you've accumulated since childhood. It's time to donate or sell. Think of it as spreading joy. That giant nutcracker might be haunting your dreams, but it could be someone else's dream come true!

And while you're at it, why not turn decluttering into a community garage or church sale? Get your neighbors or friends involved—make it a competitive sport! See who can get rid of the most tacky Santa sweaters or outdated fruitcake tins. Add some leftover holiday cookies, and you've got yourself a festive post-holiday tradition (Tagle, 2023).

Oh, and one last thing: celebrate your wins. You just conquered clutter, organized your seasonal decor, and probably burned a few calories hauling boxes around. That calls for a treat! Pour yourself a glass of anything tasty, throw on your coziest socks (maybe even matching ones), and bask in the glow of your decluttered kingdom.

Your post-holiday life doesn't have to be a battle of epic proportions. With these small hacks, you'll reclaim your home.

Chapter Summary for Busy People

Post-holiday clutter doesn't have to be a nightmare. Here are quick, practical strategies for busy parents and professionals to reclaim their space:

- **Quick, 20-minute declutters**
  - Dedicate just 20 minutes each week to tackle one clutter zone, like a drawer or shelf (Tarr, n.d.).

- **Monthly deep dives**
  - Commit to a monthly cleaning session to sort items into "keep," "donate," and "toss" piles. (Lightspeed, n.d.).

- **Seasonal reviews**
    - Every season, evaluate your belongings. Ask if you really need all those holiday mugs or if snow boots still belong in your California closet (Tagle, 2023).

- **Holiday memory box**
    - Keep sentimental holiday decor organized in a dedicated memory box, avoiding clutter while preserving memories (Walsh, 2017).

- **One-in, one-out rule from how to declutter your home in 7 simple steps**
    - The Seeker Newsmagazine Cornwall. https://theseeker.ca/2023/09/how-to-declutter-your-home-in-7-simple-steps/
    - For every new item you bring home, let go of an old one. Have you bought a new jacket? Toss the old one that's just taking up space (Zen Habits, 2008).

- **Smart storage for seasonal items**
    - Invest in proper storage solutions for holiday decorations—label boxes to avoid future chaos when looking for items (Andrea Dekker, 2024).

CHAPTER 10

Mindfulness and Minimalism: Embrace the Holiday Spirit

Embracing the holiday spirit with mindfulness and minimalism might sound as believable as a team of emperor penguins running a marathon—what a sight that would be! Picture this: instead of being buried under an avalanche of wrapping paper and decorations that look like an offensive, bad craft project, you're gliding along a peaceful river of calm and meaningful connections. The holidays don't have to be a full-blown circus with everyone vying for the biggest, shiniest toy—let's turn this into a peaceful river of calm and meaningful connections.

This chapter embarks on a fabulous journey—not a bland stroll through the mall during a last-minute shopping spree. We'll discover how practicing gratitude and mindfully letting go of excess can transform your holiday season from frantic to festive—like turning that awkward family dinner into a lively karaoke night where everyone tries to outdo each other with their questionable renditions of "Jingle Bells!"

Practice Gratitude and Letting Go of Excess

The holiday season often brings a whirlwind of activities, decorations, and material gifts. However, stepping back to cultivate gratitude can significantly shift our focus from all that shiny stuff to what truly matters—experiences, relationships, and our sanity (or lack thereof). According to *Psychology Today*, practicing gratitude can help you feel more positive about your life. Just imagine how wonderful it would be to draw closer to the holidays with a heart full of gratitude instead of a mind full of "I forgot to buy Aunt Carrol a gift!"

One effective way to nurture this mindset is by keeping a gratitude journal. In this notebook, you jot down daily reflections and thoughts that can be life-changing. For instance, instead of sulking over the latest gadget that everyone seems to have (and you still haven't got), you might write about how much you cherished that cup of coffee with your eccentric uncle who shows up every Christmas dressed as Santa. This practice helps refocus your attention on the meaningful interactions that genuinely matter while reshaping it into something that resembles a holiday miracle—like when you discover that your favorite movie is streaming on TV just when you need a break from decluttering.

Then there's the glorious art of random acts of kindness that shift our holiday priorities from a "me, me, me" mentality to generosity and compassion. Participating in charity events can be eye-opening. Whether volunteering at a soup kitchen or organizing a neighborhood coat drive, these activities provide a humbling perspective on what's truly important. They help diminish the focus on acquiring more and more things, replacing it with a sense of community and giving. Remember the time you helped serve Thanksgiving dinner at a local shelter? The warmth you felt wasn't just from the mashed potatoes but also from connecting and sharing with others.

If the holiday turmoil ever feels more than a bit overwhelming, mindfulness techniques swoop in like superheroes! Simple practices like deep breathing can ground you in the present moment, turning holiday stress into "You've Got This!" vibes. Picture this: you're frazzled from holiday shopping, feeling like a deer caught in the headlights of the county snowplow. A few deep breaths can instantly calm your mind, allowing you to actually enjoy the festive decorations around you rather than freaking out about the towering to-do list. And if anyone asks why you're staring at the ceiling, just tell them you're practicing holiday mindfulness!

Mindful Shopping and Gifting

Now, let's have a chat about mindful shopping because we all know the holidays can unleash our inner "buy-buy-buy!" beast. Instead of being lost in a whirlwind sea of stuff, let's focus on meaningful connections that ring truer than a jingle bell. Mindful shopping reduces stress and turns gift-giving into something heartfelt—think homemade cookies versus store-bought ones—because everyone wants to know you care more than just what's on sale.

One fantastic strategy for shopping mindfully is creating a thoughtful gift list. This list helps prioritize needs and desires over impulsive buying. By carefully considering the folks on your list, you can choose items that genuinely align with them. It's not about presenting a mountain of gifts but instead giving them something that'll make their eyes shine brighter than the twinkle lights on your Christmas tree. For example, did your friend dabble in gardening this year? Instead of getting them another generic gift card (because nobody remembers to use those, right?), how about a book on sustainable gardening techniques or a set of heirloom seeds? A thoughtful gift shows you put time into understanding what lights up your loved ones' faces—it's like the secret ingredient to the best holiday ever!

Now, let's discuss experiences over material items. Nothing creates memories like a cooking class where you and your sister can throw flour at each other or a hiking trip for your adventurous buddy. Experiences provide you with laughter, fun, and stories that outlive any material possessions, like a holiday postcard that everybody forgets about. Giving someone an experience is not just a nice gesture; you're gifting them a story they'll remember and retell at gatherings—pure gold! According to a study by *The Journal of Positive Psychology*, experiences create more lasting happiness than material goods. So, give the gift of laughter, not just stuff!

Supporting local artisans and shops is another excellent method of mindful shopping. Buying from local vendors doesn't just reduce your environmental impact—it supports your local economy, like when you bought supplies from your local hardware store, figured out how to fix that leaky faucet by yourself, and basically became a hero in your home.

These unique gifts are far more memorable than something off the shelf at a big box store, because let's be mindful of the fact that no one really wants another novelty coffee mug! Finding a handcrafted gift that fits perfectly in your friend's home decor is a victory!

Emphasizing quality over quantity when selecting gifts ensures they will be cherished rather than tossed aside. It's easy to get caught up in the "I need to buy x number of gifts" frenzy, but those cheap items often end up in the donation pile faster than kids unwrapping gifts. Instead, invest in higher-quality items—like a durable cast-iron skillet or a beautifully crafted leather wallet—that might cost more upfront but will be cherished for years. A lasting gift reduces waste while also being a wise investment—like a fabulous pair of shoes that never goes out of style!

Mindful shopping during the holidays isn't just about actions; it's about how we perceive and engage with the gift-giving tradition. It shifts our focus from the quantity jungle to quality treasures, making the season more intentional and fulfilling. Consider implementing these guidelines for thoughtful shopping. Next time you have a cozy cup of tea, sit down and reflect on each person, jotting down ideas that come from the heart instead of staring mindlessly at a shopping list. Writing ideas is a fantastic way to avoid those last-minute panic buys!

When purchasing physical items, consciously support local artisans and shops. Take a leisurely stroll through local markets and discover unique items that capture your community's charm. Lastly, remember to prioritize quality over quantity because, at the end of the day, your loved ones will appreciate knowing you invested thoughtfulness into their gifts!

Simplify Holiday Traditions and Rituals

Holiday seasons can sometimes feel like a whirlwind of joy wrapped in a layer of stress topped with a sprinkle of out-and-out madness. Reducing the complexity of your holiday traditions helps foster a relaxed and joyful environment. Let's delve into how we can simplify our festive routines while still keeping the season's spirit alive!

First, let's rethink those traditional activities. Ever find yourself dreading baking ten types of cookies each year, only for half to end up in the back of the freezer watching old movies? It might be time to drop the cookie selection down to your three favorite family recipes—

because who needs cookie-related stress? You'll reduce kitchen dread, allowing you to actually enjoy the process rather than stressing from kitchen timer anxiety!

Collaborative celebrations are another way to lighten the load. Ditch the myth that one person has to shoulder all the holiday hosting responsibilities. Instead, let's potluck! Each guest brings a dish, easing the burden on the main host and turning meals into a delightful treasure trove of flavors. Plus, who doesn't want to show off their signature dish? Just hope Aunt Debbie doesn't bring her infamous fruitcake again. Another fun idea is to have each guest or family make and bring a side dish never heard of or tried by the group. You just might discover an amazing new dish and incorporate it into next year's festivities. Suggestions would be to have guests bring an internationally unknown dish, a family heritage dish from the early century, or even a new dish just created. It's all about new experiences, playful competition, and, of course, lots of laughter.

Then we have decorations—those delightful little things that can quickly turn a cozy living room into what looks like a warehouse that snorted glitter. Focus on a few cherished items to create a peaceful and intentional aesthetic. Imagine a beautifully decorated tree adorned with cherished ornaments rather than a full-blown Christmas store extravaganza! Mindful decor decorating evokes nostalgia and peace rather than making it feel like you stepped into a holiday yard sale.

Setting specific times for traditions can ease stress and manage expectations. Designate specific days for activities—one for tree decorating, another for holiday movie marathons, and maybe even one for baking (thank goodness!) so grandma doesn't end up buried under mountains of bread dough, cookie dough, and pie crusts. Spreading out activities allows everyone to fully engage without racing towards the finish line, creating a festive atmosphere without panic.

New, simpler rituals can be just as rewarding as their traditional counterparts. How about a weekly board game night or a leisurely evening walk through the neighborhood to admire the twinkling lights? These new traditions don't need grand setups; they offer quality family time and an opportunity to unwind together! In addition to simplifying activities and decorations, a minimalist take on gift-giving can alleviate significant stress.

How about stirring up some holiday fun with a Secret Santa exchange among adults instead of buying presents for every family member? Secret Santa Exchanges doesn't just cut down on shopping time (and expenses) but also adds an element of surprise! Imagine the delightful fun as everyone unwraps their gifts, hoping their thoughtful Secret Santa didn't mistakenly gift them the world's largest snow globe—or worse, another set of socks or a tie.

Less Is More: The Joy of Minimalism

In a world where excess often masquerades as success, minimalism can feel like a breath of fresh air—like walking into a cozy cabin after spending too long in a crowded shopping mall. When we embrace minimalism during the holidays, we prioritize what truly matters— family, experiences, and memories—over a mountain of material goods.

Consider your home during the holidays. How often do you pull out decorations only to realize that half are broken or tangled in a web of lights, and you haven't used them since the last millennium? Simplifying your decor doesn't mean turning into the Grinch; instead, it means focusing on what sparks joy—because those reindeer that sing "Jingle Bells" are probably more terrifying than delightful at this point! Instead, select a few items that evoke warm memories and create a festive atmosphere without turning your living room into a theme park for Christmas cheer.

Minimalism also allows us to consider what we truly need. Do you really want to gift your cousin a bunch of random gadgets they'll never use, or would a heartfelt letter expressing your gratitude and love for them mean more? Not only does it save you the stress of shopping, but it also offers a chance to connect deeply with those you love.

According to *The Minimalists*, embracing minimalism can lead to more fulfilling relationships and increased happiness. So why not focus on spending quality time with loved ones instead of getting caught in the consumerist trap? Plan game nights, movie marathons, or even DIY gift-making parties where everyone can create something special for each other. It's about creating shared experiences that strengthen your bonds and give you stories to tell for years to come—like the time Uncle Bob attempted to bake cookies and somehow invented a new form of a kitchen blow torch that even the smoke detector couldn't handle.

Mindful Eating During the Holidays

Ah, holiday feasting—an event as eagerly anticipated as a surprise snow day! But even this joyous occasion can become overwhelming if not approached with mindfulness. Rather than treating meals as a "see how much I can pile on my plate" contest, let's savor each bite as if it were a little holiday miracle.

Start by preparing and enjoying food together, transforming cooking from a chore into a festive gathering. Cooking with loved ones creates cherished memories and invites laughter—just be prepared for someone to inevitably burn the cookies (sorry, Aunt Ruth!). Kitchen mishaps can lead to an unexpected baking showdown where everyone pretends their charred offerings are actually gourmet delights.

Mindful eating helps us appreciate what's in front of us. Instead of gobbling down your meal while scrolling through social media (because who can resist the allure of holiday cat videos?), take the time to enjoy the flavors, textures, and aromas. Each mouthful should be a mini celebration of gratitude for the effort put into making the meal.

Portion control can be a helpful ally in this journey. Try serving smaller portions instead of piling your plate high enough to rival the Empire State Building. Smaller portions help you to enjoy a wider variety of dishes without feeling like you just finished a triathlon and prevent the food coma that follows overeating. As *Harvard Health* suggests, smaller portions lead to healthier eating habits and better digestion, meaning you can still enjoy dessert without feeling like a stuffed turkey!

Let's not forget about the joys of leftovers. As you clear away your holiday feast, consider how much food often goes to waste. Plan meals creatively using leftovers instead of letting perfectly good food deteriorate or ferment in the fridge. After all, who doesn't love a good turkey sandwich with cranberry sauce?

Navigate Family Dynamics With Humor

Holidays and family gatherings can sometimes feel like a combination of a circus and a soap opera. Family members often come together with differing opinions, personalities, and quirks that can lead to tension. But rather than dreading the annual gathering, why not embrace it with humor?

When the conversation shifts to that sensitive topic—politics, religion, or Aunt Karen's third husband—remember that laughter is the best medicine. Sharing funny stories about past family gatherings can help lighten the mood. For instance, recall the time Cousin Jimmy tried to impress everyone with his "expert" turkey carving skills and created a masterpiece that looked suspiciously like a horror movie prop.

A humorous approach to these interactions can transform awkward situations into hilarious memories. If Uncle Fred starts lecturing everyone on his latest conspiracy theory, you might respond with a deadpan, "Have you considered starting a podcast? You'd go viral!" Humor can diffuse tension and steer conversations into lighter territory, fostering a more enjoyable gathering.

One way to maintain balance during the family festivities is to set boundaries. It's perfectly okay to excuse yourself from conversations that spiral into negativity. Politely redirect discussions or step outside for a breather, perhaps while admiring the neighbor's extravagant light display—because who hasn't wondered how their electric bill must look after all those twinkling decorations?

Ultimately, remember that family dynamics don't have to resemble a battlefield. Approach interactions with empathy and a sprinkle of humor, reminding yourself that everyone is human and can get a little wacky during the holidays. You'll leave the gathering with more than just full bellies—you'll have shared laughter and strengthened bonds.

The Magic of Presence: Mindfulness in the Moment

As we navigate through the holidays, let's embrace the magic of presence—because nothing quite says "I'm here" like being genuinely engaged with those around you. It's easy to get swept away in the hustle and bustle, but practicing mindfulness reminds us to stay grounded in the moment.

Start by setting aside technology during family gatherings. We're all guilty of sneaking a peek at our phones when we should be engaging with our loved ones. Set a communal phone box at the door where everyone can deposit their devices upon arrival. This small act will foster connection and conversation, turning the event into a delightful reunion rather than a series of disconnected moments where everyone is busy scrolling.

Encourage everyone to share stories and memories. Perhaps you'll discover that your grandmother once played in a rock band or that your cousin spent a summer living in a van while traveling the country. These shared moments create a tapestry of experiences that deepen relationships and remind us of the joy of connection.

During meals, engage in gratitude circles where everyone shares something they're thankful for that year. This practice fosters an environment of appreciation, creating a sense of community that resonates far beyond the holiday table. You might even hear Uncle George say he's grateful for finding his favorite pair of socks from last year's Christmas!

A Season of Joy and Simplicity

As we draw this chapter to a close, remember that the holiday season doesn't have to be a chaotic whirlwind filled with stress, excess, and awkward family gatherings. Instead, it can be a time of joy, connection, and simplicity, embracing the true spirit of the season. By practicing mindfulness, letting go of excess, and prioritizing meaningful interactions, you'll create a holiday experience that warms your heart like a cozy cup of cocoa.

So, let's ditch the notion that we need to impress anyone with extravagant displays or endless gift lists. Instead, let's focus on creating joyful memories with our loved ones—whether that means sharing a laugh over burnt cookies, gifting experiences rather than material items, or simply enjoying each other's company without distractions. The holidays are meant to be a time of love, laughter, and gratitude, and with a mindful approach, we can transform them into something truly magical.

As the holidays roll in like a glitter-covered freight train, remember that less can be more. It's not about how many lights you can string up before the neighbors file a complaint—it's about the twinkle in your loved one's eyes and not in the plastic reindeer on your lawn. The real magic happens in the moments of laughter, the warmth of togetherness, and the memories that don't come from a sale rack.

Chapter Summary for Busy People

- **Embrace the holiday spirit mindfully:** Instead of feeling overwhelmed by decorations and shopping, focus on creating calm, meaningful connections with loved ones.

- **Practice gratitude:** Shift focus from material things to experiences and relationships by keeping a gratitude journal and savoring interactions.

- **Random acts of kindness:** Participate in charitable activities to foster community spirit and reduce the focus on consumerism.

Mindful Shopping and Gifting

- **Create a thoughtful gift list:** Focus on meaningful, personalized gifts rather than impulsive purchases.

- **Prioritize experiences over material goods:** Gifts like shared activities (e.g., classes, trips) create lasting memories and happiness.

- **Support local vendors:** Buying from small, local businesses supports the economy and provides unique, memorable gifts.

- **Emphasize quality over quantity:** Thoughtful, durable items are cherished longer than cheap, forgettable gifts.

Simplifying Holiday Traditions

- **Rethink holiday activities:** Simplify traditions to reduce stress (e.g., baking fewer cookie types or delegating holiday meal prep).

- **Declutter decorations:** Focus on sentimental items for a peaceful, intentional aesthetic.

- **Set designated times for traditions:** Spread out activities to avoid rushing and create a relaxed, festive atmosphere.

Minimalism and Joy

- **Less is more:** Focus on meaningful interactions rather than material possessions, such as organizing Secret Santa exchanges or sharing personal letters.

- **Minimize holiday decor:** Select a few cherished items to create a warm, festive environment without excess clutter.

Mindful Eating

- **Enjoy food mindfully:** Slow down, savor each bite, and avoid overeating by serving smaller portions and appreciating the meal with loved ones.

- **Creative use of leftovers:** Plan meals with leftovers to minimize food waste.

Navigating Family Dynamics With Humor

- **Handle awkward conversations with humor:** Defuse tense moments by redirecting the topic with lighthearted jokes or humor.

- **Set boundaries:** Politely excuse yourself from negative conversations and focus on enjoyable interactions.

The Magic of Presence

- **Be present:** Set aside technology during gatherings to foster real connections and conversations.

- **Encourage storytelling and gratitude:** Share memories and express gratitude to deepen relationships and create lasting bonds.

Conclusion

Simplify for joy: Focus on what truly matters—love, laughter, and shared experiences—over extravagant displays or endless gift lists. A mindful approach brings more joy to the holiday season.

Chapter 11:

Decluttering the Basement: An Adventure in Two Acts

Ah, the basement. That mystical land beneath your house where holiday decorations, forgotten treasures, and the occasional unwelcomed field mouse reign supreme. It's where Halloween skeletons hide year-round, and you're pretty sure the Easter Bunny set up camp with Santa Claus next to the tangled Christmas lights. So, what happens when the time comes to reclaim this subterranean wilderness? Whether your basement is a finished living space or an unfinished cave of mystery, we are going in like brave souls to declutter and clean your holiday objects.

Scenario 1: The Empty Basement of Holiday Cheer

Imagine this: your basement is a blank canvas, eagerly awaiting the brush strokes of holiday cheer. But before you dive headfirst into an avalanche of glittery decorations and seasonal objects, let's channel the minimalist wisdom of Joshua Fields Millburn and Ryan Nicodemus. These two authors, known for living a meaningful life with less stuff, emphasize the benefits of decluttering. So, let's avoid transforming this space into a holiday landfill!

Step 1: Gather Your Supplies

First things first: you need supplies. Not just any supplies—decluttering supplies! Gather bins, boxes, and maybe a snack (because we all know the importance of sustaining life when facing the abyss of clutter). As Marie Kondo, author of *The Life-Changing Magic of Tidying Up*, suggests, it's crucial to keep only the items that "spark joy." So, prepare to wield your joy-o-meter like a true decluttering warrior.

Step 2: Sort Like a Pro

Next, sort your holiday decorations into categories: lights, ornaments, garlands, and that mysterious "What in the world is this?" pile. You know the one—it's filled with items you bought at the post-holiday sale, thinking they'd be useful but have since become ancient relics. Use Kondo's method to determine what truly brings joy. Does that glittery elf from 2003 still make you smile, or does it make you question your life choices? If it doesn't spark joy, toss it into the donation box faster than you can say, "What was I thinking?"

Step 3: Clean up the Mess

Now that you've sorted your stuff, it's time to clean the basement. Grab a broom, a mop, and perhaps some industrial-strength cleaning supplies. If things are particularly bleak, you might even want to wear a hazmat suit. Give the space a good scrub to ensure your festive decorations have a clean, welcoming home. This is a great opportunity to improve mental clarity and reduce stress. According to *Harvard Health Publishing*, a clean environment can lead to improved mental well-being. Plus, you won't be inhaling decades-old dust while hanging your ornaments!

Step 4: Organize Like a Boss

Once the space is clean, it's time to organize. Invest in sturdy shelving or clear bins—because nothing says "I've got my life together" like organized holiday decor. Label the bins so you won't find yourself diving into a pile of tinsel while searching for your precious holiday lights. Practical tips from *Good Housekeeping* suggest utilizing vertical space and stacking bins to maximize storage. Who knew that organizing could make you feel like a superhero?

Step 5: Enjoy Your Holiday Bliss

With your basement decluttered and organized, it's time to decorate without the holiday chaos weighing you down. A clean space enhances your decorating experience and can reduce holiday-related anxiety. Remember, it's all about creating joyful memories, not just accumulating stuff.

Scenario 2: The Finished Basement of Festive Fun

Now, let's shift gears. Picture this: your finished basement is not just a storage space but also a cozy family area—where you enjoy movie nights, host game tournaments, and occasionally use it as a temporary holiday storage facility. The good news? You can declutter while keeping the festive fun intact!

Step 1: Assess the Space

Start by assessing your finished basement. Determine which areas you will dedicate to holiday storage and which are for everyday use. You'll want to keep the living space functional while managing holiday decorations. It's essential to maintain some semblance of order amidst the chaos. After all, according to *Psychology Today*, clutter can impact mental health, so let's avoid any unnecessary meltdowns over where the remote went this holiday season!

Step 2: Create Holiday Zones

Designate specific areas for your holiday decorations. Consider creating a holiday corner that includes a shelf for decorations and a bin for wrapping supplies. Stand-alone storage or pantry cabinets are another option. Embrace the holiday spirit without sacrificing the coziness of your finished basement!

Step 3: Sort, Simplify, and Simplify Again

Use the Kondo method again—this time for your finished space. Evaluate each item's joy factor. Does that inflatable Santa add to your life, or does it make you question your decisions? If it makes you question your life, toss it into the donation pile quicker than you can say "holiday horror story."

Step 4: Embrace Vertical Storage

Take advantage of vertical space to keep your finished basement from looking like a post-holiday war zone. Install shelves for decorations and use bins to store seasonal items out of sight. This will keep your living area tidy while allowing for festive flair when the holidays roll around. Bonus points if you can label them in an artsy, Pinterest-worthy way—just remember to keep it realistic!

Step 5: Make it a Family Affair

Involve the whole family in the decluttering process. Make it a fun activity—put on holiday music and have everyone join in on the sorting. After all, what's more festive than a family bonding experience filled with laughter and a little bit of mess? As you all declutter together, share stories about the items you're considering keeping. Storytelling could lighten the mood and foster family bonding, transforming the chore into a cherished memory.

Step 6: Celebrate Your Success

Once you finish organizing your basement, take a moment to celebrate. Light some candles, grab some hot cocoa, and enjoy the newfound space you've created. A clean, organized area may lead to improved mental well-being. Remember, a tidy space is a happy space!

The Magical Transformation

Now that we've tackled the clutter, let's take a moment to revel in the transformation. Picture this: a bright, organized basement where every ornament has a home, every strand of lights is untangled, and every family member is smiling instead of searching for their favorite decoration. It's the stuff holiday dreams are made of!

Step 7: Master the Art of Holiday Decor Rotation

Here's a fun idea: consider a rotation system instead of keeping every holiday decoration known to humankind. This way, you can enjoy different decorations each year without the overwhelming clutter. Think of it as a seasonal surprise party for your basement! Just be sure to journal or note what you put away and where you stored it—because trying to remember where you stashed the inflatable snowman from last year is like searching for a needle in a haystack.

The Unwritten Rule of Holiday Decorating

There's an unwritten rule about holiday decorating: the earlier you start, the more likely you are to avoid the holiday panic. So why not embrace the spirit early? Get those decorations out while you have the time and energy. After all, nothing screams "I'm on top of my holiday game," like decorating your home in November. Just beware, there are those in the northern states that joke snow happens in November because "Some of you prematurely decorated for Christmas." They go on to say, "You know who you are. Knock it off."

A Word From the Professionals

Incorporate wisdom from professional organizers like Peter Walsh, who advises that decluttering isn't just about cleaning for cleaning's sake; it's about creating a space that reflects your values and lifestyle. Similarly, the NEAT Method team, including Ashley Murphy and Molly Graves, emphasizes the importance of thoughtful organization. They suggest decluttering and ensuring that your space serves you well.

Embrace Minimalism During the Holidays

The holidays can often become a time of excess, but adopting a minimalist approach can lead to a more meaningful experience. *The Minimalists* advocate for living with less, which can be particularly beneficial during this season. Instead of focusing on the quantity of decorations, consider the quality. Choose pieces that resonate with you and your family. This way, you can enjoy the holiday spirit without the burden of excess.

The Psychological Benefits of a Decluttered Space

As noted in various studies by *Psychology Today*, clutter can significantly impact mental health. By decluttering your basement and creating an organized space, you're not just improving your physical surroundings; you're also enhancing your mental well-being.

Tidy Up With Joy

Marie Kondo's approach, rooted in the philosophy of only keeping what "sparks joy," is especially relevant during the holidays. Take the time to truly appreciate each decoration. Does that vintage ornament bring back cherished memories of family gatherings? Keep it. Does that questionable light-up Santa just remind you of awkward office parties? It might be time to let it go. Embrace the joy in your decorations!

Create a Holiday Planning System

To make the most of your organized space, create a holiday planning system. Designate a spot for a holiday calendar, a checklist for decorating, and a list of family traditions you want to maintain. This way, you can keep everything in one place, reducing the chances of holiday havoc sneaking in.

Turn Clutter Into Creativity

If you have kids, encourage them to get creative with holiday decorating. Instead of relying solely on store-bought decorations. Have some quality family time and have fun crafting homemade ornaments or decorations. You might end up with some bizarre creations, but those quirky additions will make your holiday decor truly unique. And hey, if nothing else, you'll have a great story to tell during family gatherings!

The Holiday Hangover: Post-Season Decluttering

As the holidays wrap up, remember that decluttering doesn't stop once the decorations go up. After the festivities, it's crucial to evaluate what you've accumulated. Do a quick post-holiday audit of your basement. Toss any items that no longer serve a purpose or that your family has outgrown. This little tweak will help keep your basement organized year-round.

The Gift of a Clutter-Free Basement

Whether you have an empty basement waiting to be transformed into a holiday wonderland or a finished basement that doubles as a cozy hangout spot, decluttering for the holidays doesn't have to be a stressful endeavor. By following these steps and incorporating joy, organization, and a little humor into the process, you'll turn your basement from a cluttered mess into a festive space where holiday memories can truly thrive.

So grab those decorations, sprinkle some cheer, and get ready for the most organized holiday season yet! Remember, your basement can be a magical place of joy and laughter—if you can only find it beneath the chaos. Now go forth and declutter, my festive friends!

Chapter Summary for Busy People

- **Step 1: Gather supplies**
  - Collect decluttering tools: bins, boxes, and snacks.
  - Follow Marie Kondo's *spark joy* philosophy: keep only items that bring you happiness.

- **Step 2: Sort holiday decorations**
  - Create categories for decorations (lights, ornaments, garlands, etc.).
  - Sort out unused or outdated items—don't keep anything that doesn't make you smile.

- **Step 3: Clean the basement**
  - Sweep, mop and dust to ensure the space is fresh for your holiday decorations.
  - Remember: a clean environment improves mental clarity and reduces stress (Harvard Health).

- **Step 4: Organize decorations**
  - Invest in shelving and clear bins to store and label holiday items.
  - Use vertical storage to maximize space and keep things tidy (Good Housekeeping).

- **Step 5: Enjoy a clutter-free space**
  - Now that your basement is decluttered, decorating becomes stress-free.

- A clean space enhances your holiday mood and reduces anxiety.

Scenario 2: Finished Basement With Festive Fun

- **Step 1: Assess the space**
    - Determine which parts of your basement are for storage and which are for everyday activities.
    - Keep clutter away to maintain mental well-being (Psychology Today).
- **Step 2: Create holiday zones**
    - Designate specific areas for holiday decor storage without sacrificing the coziness of your living space.
- **Step 3: Sort and simplify**
    - Use Marie Kondo's method again—if a decoration doesn't bring joy, let it go!
- **Step 4: Maximize vertical space**
    - Use shelves and bins to keep seasonal items organized and out of sight.
- **Step 5: Involve the family**
    - Turn decluttering into a fun family activity by sharing stories about holiday items and listening to festive music.
- **Step 6: Celebrate your success**
    - Light candles, sip cocoa, and enjoy the clean, organized space.
    - A decluttered environment can improve your mental well-being and holiday experience.

- **Rotate holiday decorations**

  - Instead of keeping everything, rotate decorations each year to keep things fresh.

- **Start decorating early**

  - Avoid holiday panic by pulling out your decorations well before the season starts.

- **Expert advice**

  - Peter Walsh says decluttering reflects your values; ensure your space aligns with how you want to live.

  - The NEAT Method emphasizes functional organization and thoughtful storage solutions.

- **Minimalism and holiday cheer**

  - The Minimalists encourage focusing on meaningful decorations, reducing the burden of excess clutter during the holidays.

- **Post-holiday decluttering**

  - After the season ends, evaluate which decorations are worth keeping. Toss or donate those that no longer serve a purpose.

CHAPTER 12

From Clutter to Clarity: Revel in Your Holiday Decluttering Triumph

As you plop down on the couch and take a well-earned breath, let's take a moment to celebrate what you've accomplished—not just in clearing out your space but in transforming your life. Yes, it might have felt like you were waging war against an army of plastic Tupperware lids, sentimental knick-knacks, and that mysterious drawer full of cables that fit absolutely nothing you own. But you did it! And you didn't just survive—you thrived.

Gone are the days when you had to play a twisted version of Jenga every time you opened a closet or sidestep piles of clutter like you're competing in some bizarre home obstacle course. Remember that feeling when you'd enter a room and think, *Where do I even start?* Well, take a look around now. Every drawer, every closet, every corner— now conquered! You've not only made space in your home but in your mind, too. It's like you've deleted 1,000 unread emails from your brain's inbox. Ah, the freedom!

But let's be honest: this wasn't just about shoving stuff into boxes labeled "Donate" and "Mystery Junk I'll Never Use Again." Decluttering is a journey—a mindset, really. You've gone from someone who may have once clung to that novelty mug collection from your college days like it was a retirement plan to someone who asks, "Does this truly serve a purpose in my life?" And that, my friend, is pure decluttering enlightenment.

Along the way, you've learned the magic of living with less. Marie Kondo would be proud—you've asked the "Does it spark joy?"

question more times than you ever thought possible, and you've honed your ability to let go of things that no longer serve you. And if you've tossed out items that *might* have sparked a little less joy than they once did, that's growth!

Speaking of growth, let's not forget the emotional weight you've shed along with the clutter. As we've learned, clutter can mess with your mental health, according to Psychology Today, and clutter is a sneaky culprit that raises stress levels and hijacks your sense of peace. Harvard Health Publishing even links decluttering to improved mental clarity and reduced anxiety. It's science, people! So, as you cleared those shelves and organized those closets, you weren't just tidying up—you were giving yourself the gift of mental wellness.

Of course, no decluttering journey is complete without a nod to the sentimental items you bravely tackled. Whether it was your kid's first-grade artwork (all 2,743 pieces of it) or the stack of old Christmas cards from people you haven't spoken to in a decade, you made some tough decisions. Sure, it was a little heartbreaking at first, but now you've got space for the things that *truly* matter. And isn't it liberating to know that your memories aren't tied to things but to the moments those things represent?

I'd be lying if I said this was a solo mission. Decluttering isn't just about you—it's about your family, too. Getting everyone on board wasn't easy, I know. Convincing a child to part with that stuffed animal they haven't touched in three years? That's practically Olympic-level parenting. But you did it together, and now everyone gets to enjoy the benefits of a clutter-free home. Plus, you've taught them valuable lessons about mindfulness and simplicity that will stick with them longer than that random action figure with one missing arm ever could.

So, what's next? Like any major life change, maintaining this new, organized way of living requires a little upkeep. But now you've got the tools and the mindset to handle it. Remember how good it feels to have a space that works *for* you, not against you. The next time you're tempted to let clutter creep back in (because, let's face it, clutter is sneaky), you'll know exactly how to shut it down before it takes over again.

And when you find yourself in a store surrounded by shiny gadgets and unnecessary doodads, channel your inner minimalist. The Minimalists, Joshua Fields Millburn and Ryan Nicodemus, would remind you that life is about living with intention, not filling your home with things you don't need. Just because it's on sale doesn't mean it belongs in your life or storage bins.

Oh, and let's not forget the holiday things! Yes, the holidays—when decorations and gift wrap tend to multiply like rabbits. But this year, you'll approach them with the calm, centered grace of someone who has mastered the art of decluttering. Thanks to Good Housekeeping's seasonal organizing tips and the wisdom of experts like Ashley Murphy and Molly Graves from NEAT Method, you now know how to manage holiday goods without turning your living spaces into a storage disaster zone.

In the end, decluttering is about more than just tidying up. It's about creating space for what really matters—peace, joy, and a sense of control over your surroundings. You've decluttered your home, mind, and holiday storage bins. So go ahead, give yourself a well-deserved pat on the back, maybe pour yourself a glass of wine, or take an uninterrupted nap (because, hey, you can actually *find* your bed now). You've done something incredible.

And remember, as Marie Kondo herself might say, "The space you live in should be for the person you are becoming now, not for the person you were in the past." So embrace that person with clear counters and clutter-free closets, and live your best, most joyful, most organized life.

Conclusion: A Season of Joy and Simplicity

As we draw this chapter to a close, remember that the holiday season doesn't have to be a gigantic whirlwind filled with stress, excess, and awkward family gatherings. Instead, it can be a time of joy, connection, and simplicity, embracing the true spirit of the season. Practicing mindfulness, letting go of excess, and prioritizing meaningful interactions will create a holiday experience that warms your heart like a cozy cup of cocoa.

So, let's ditch the notion that we need to impress anyone with extravagant displays or endless gift lists. Instead, let's focus on creating joyful memories with our loved ones—whether that means sharing a laugh over burnt cookies, gifting experiences rather than material items, or simply enjoying each other's company without distractions. The holidays are meant to be a time of love, laughter, and gratitude, and with a mindful approach, we can transform them into something truly magical. The real magic happens in the moments of laughter, the warmth of togetherness, and *not* the memories that come from malls or box stores. So ditch the clutter and focus on the things that actually matter—because no gadget ever hugged you back or told a funny story at the dinner table.

Chapter Summary for Busy People

- **Celebrate your progress:** You've not just decluttered your home but transformed your life.

- **Tame the chaos:** No more playing closet Jenga or dodging piles of clutter.

- **Mind and space:** Decluttering your home also clears your mind—like deleting 1,000 unread emails.

- **Decluttering mindset:** It's more than organizing; it's a lifestyle shift, focusing on purpose and value.

- **Growth through letting go:** You've learned to release items that no longer serve you.

- **Mental wellness:** Decluttering improves mental clarity and reduces stress, supported by research from *Psychology Today* and *Harvard Health Publishing*.

- **Sentimental items:** You've tackled the emotional challenges of parting with sentimental things.

- **Family teamwork:** You got everyone involved, even teaching mindfulness and simplicity to your loved ones.

- **Ongoing maintenance:** Stay mindful to keep clutter from sneaking back into your life.

- **Smart shopping:** Avoid buying unnecessary items just because they're on sale—be intentional.

- **Holiday approach:** Apply your decluttering skills to keep the holidays stress-free and focused on meaningful moments.

- **Create space for joy:** You've made room for peace, joy, and control over your surroundings.

- **Living intentionally:** Embrace the person you are becoming—organized, peaceful, and clutter-free.

References

360-admin, newlife. (2021, December 31). 4 common mental and emotional issues during the holidays – new life 360°. *Newlife360inc.com.* https://newlife360inc.com/blog/holiday-depression

Admin. (2023, October 7). *Bulk christmas gift boxes: Spreading holiday magic, one box at a time - games of sports and toto.* Games of Sports and Toto. https://gamesofsportsandtoto.com/bulk-christmas-gift-boxes-spreading-holiday-magic-one-box-at-a-time/

Admin, M. S. (2024, March 26). How to declutter your kitchen: A step-by-step plan. *Vertical Spice.* https://verticalspice.com/blogs/news/how-to-declutter-your-kitchen?

Bennett, J. (2021, December 21). *27 no-fail tricks for arranging furniture in every room.* Better Homes & Gardens. https://www.bhg.com/decorating/lessons/basics/how-to-arrange-furniture/

Bloss, J. (2023, December 4). *17 genius organizers that will keep all your gift-wrapping supplies neat and tidy | CNN Underscored.* CNN Underscored. https://www.cnn.com/cnn-underscored/home/best-wrapping-paper-storage-organizers

CoCo. (2023, February 20). *How to organize your kitchen into work-friendly zones.* Thecrownedgoat.com. https://thecrownedgoat.com/how-to-organize-your-kitchen-into-work-friendly-zones/

COOK, K. (2023, November 16). *Create a kitchen that serves up joy in time for the holidays.* AP News. https://apnews.com/article/kitchen-design-happy-vibes-66ea399ae0702119d2a4680cd5219d07

Counts, E. (2019, December 11). *An organized wrapping paper storage bin - small stuff counts.* Small Stuff Counts. https://smallstuffcounts.com/wrapping-paper-storage-bin/

Create your own gift wrapping station - holiday shopping | holiday gifts & lifestyle special section. (2024). Metrocreativeconnection.com.

https://mcg.metrocreativeconnection.com/publish/sections/demos/TF12
12-HolidayGiftsLifestyle/article0021.html

Dolorese Mukisa. (2022, March 13). *A minimalist easter: Easter tablescape decor ideas.* FLOURISHED MINIMALIST. https://flourishedminimalist.com/a-minimalist-easter-easter-tablescape-decor-ideas/

Harvard Health. (n.d.). Www.health.harvard.edu. https://www.health.harvard.edu/mind-and-mood/

heidis. (2023, August 17). *Simple and charming minimalist fall decor ideas.* Eleanor Rose Home. https://eleanorrosehome.com/2023/08/17/minimalist-fall-decor/

Hines, R. (2019, June 28). *See britney spears channel her "...Baby one more time" look 21 years later.* TODAY.com; TODAY. https://www.today.com/home/how-organize-pro-neat-method-s-founders-ashley-murphy-molly-t157419

https://www.facebook.com/AndreaDekkerDOTcom. (2024, February 14). *Love it, use it, or lose it - your simple decluttering guide.* Andrea Dekker. https://andreadekker.com/love-it-use-it-or-lose-it

Index of blogs. (n.d.). *Psychology Today.* https://www.psychologytoday.com/us/blog/

Jones, I. (2023, September 12). *How to declutter your home in 7 simple steps.* The Seeker. https://theseeker.ca/2023/09/how-to-declutter-your-home-in-7-simple-steps/

Kerr, J. (2022, December 5). *26 clever holiday decoration storage ideas, according to organizing experts.* CNN Underscored; CNN Underscored. https://www.cnn.com/cnn-underscored/home/holiday-decoration-storage-tips-essentials

Kramer, J., & Kelly, A. (2024, February 2). *How to arrange your furniture to give your home the best flow.* Martha Stewart. https://www.marthastewart.com/2219858/how-arrange-furniture-best-flow-through-home

LaScala, M., & Freedman, A. (2017, October 5). *55 best Halloween movies for kids and families.* Good Housekeeping. https://www.goodhousekeeping.com/home/organizing/tips/g2661/holiday-decor-storage.

Lawson, A. (2021, September 21). How to create a whole house uniform. *Abby Organizes.* https://justagirlandherblog.com/how-to-buy-less-decor/

Mindful Decluttering & Organizing, LLC. (2019, October 12). Reduce food waste and kitchen stress through organizing. *Mindful Decluttering & Organizing.* https://clutterfreenow.com/blog/decluttering-and-organizing-tips/how-to-reduce-food-waste-and-kitchen-stress-through-organizing/

mindset, decluttering. (2022). *How decluttering makes holidays fun again! – the decluttering corner*. Thedeclutteringcorner.com. https://thedeclutteringcorner.com/how-decluttering-makes-holidays-fun-again/

Minimalists, T. (2018). *The minimalists*. The Minimalists. https://www.theminimalists.com

Nast, C. (2016a, January 8). *33 best closet organization ideas to maximize space and style*. Architectural Digest. https://www.architecturaldigest.com/gallery/how-to-organize-your-closet

Nast, C. (2016b, January 8). *33 best closet organization ideas to maximize space and style*. Architectural Digest. https://www.architecturaldigest.com/gallery/how-to-organize-your-closet

Nicasio, F. (2024, June 11). *11 stockroom organization ideas and guidelines to implement in your retail store*. Lightspeed. https://www.lightspeedhq.com/blog/retail-stockroom-organization-ideas/

Poplin, J. (2019, October 11). *The 7 best things to declutter before the holidays - the simplicity habit*. The Simplicity Habit. https://www.thesimplicityhabit.com/the-best-things-to-declutter-before-the-holidays/

Roberts, D. (2024). The resilient brain. *Psychology Today*. https://www.psychologytoday.com/us/blog/the-resilient-brain/

Simple, R. (n.d.). *Log into Facebook*. Facebook. https://www.facebook.com/realsimple.

Stamp, E. (2020, May 19). *20 kitchen organization ideas to maximize storage space*. Architectural Digest. https://www.architecturaldigest.com/story/kitchen-organization-ideas-to-maximize-storage-space

Tagle, A. (2023, January 3). *The decluttering philosophy that can help you keep your home organized*. NPR; NPR. https://www.npr.org/2022/12/19/1144110063/clear-out-your-clutter

Tarr, C. (n.d.). 18 warehouse organization ideas to boost productivity and morale. *Us.blog.kardex-Remstar.com*. https://us.blog.kardex-remstar.com/warehouse-organization-ideas

Team, UR. Life. (2023). *Decluttering your space For the festive season*. UR.Life. https://ur.life/article/decluttering-your-space-for-the-festive-season

US, K. (2023, October 3). *Keeping your holiday decor organized and clean in your storage shed*. Keter.com. https://www.keter.com/en-us/inspiration/keeping-your-holiday-decor-organized-and-clean-in-your-storage-shed.html

Walsh, P. (2017, March 16). *Peter Walsh strategies for getting rid of clutter*. Oprah.com; Oprah.com. https://www.oprah.com/home/peter-walsh-strategies-for-getting-rid-of-clutter

Wang, W. (2023, October 28). Simplify and store: The ultimate guide to easy-to-store christmas decor. *F&J Outdoors; F&J Outdoors*. https://fj-outdoors.com/blogs/guide/simplify-and-store-the-ultimate-guide-to-easy-to-store-christmas-decor

Why cluttered kitchens are costing you time. (n.d.). *Prochefkitchentools.com*. https://prochefkitchentools.com/blogs/tips/why_cluttered_kitchens_are_costing_you_time

Wright, N. C. P. O. T., Organization, O. H., Organization, O., Services, L. O., Taya, in addition to interior styling services to residents across the G. H. area W. with, website, her team is easy Y. can book an appointment easily on her, & at 832-271-7608, O. C. H. D. (2023, November 13). *Eco-friendly elegance: Sustainable home decorating and home organization tips | just organized by Taya.* https://justorganized.org/eco-friendly-elegance-sustainable-home-decorating-and-home-organization-tips/

zenhabits. (2008, November 19). *Living simply: The ultimate guide to conquering your clutter*. Zen Habits. https://zenhabits.net/living-simply-the-ultimate-guide-to-conquering-your-clutter/